CHILDREN AT THE LORD'S TABLE

CHILDREN AT THE LORD'S TABLE

JOHN T. HINANT

CHILDREN AT THE LORD'S TABLE
Copyright © 2005 by John T. Hinant

All rights reserved. This book, or parts thereof, may not be reprinted in any form without permission of the author, except in the case of brief quotations included in critical articles and reviews.

Cover and Interior Design: Robert Coalson

Contact: eleyce.hinant@verizon.net

Published by: Three Fountains Publishing

ISBN 0-9777889-0-3

SAN 850-2447
Three Fountains Publishing
Indianapolis, Indiana

Printed in the United States of America

Dedication

This book is gratefully dedicated to the children about whom Jesus said, "Let the children come unto me and forbid them not."

Preface

As a young minister in the early 1960's, parent of two young children and a student in the Institute for Child Study at the University of Maryland, I considered myself knowledgeable regarding children's spiritual development, sensitive to their needs and an advocate for their well being. It therefore came as a shock to discover that I was neither as knowledgeable, sensitive or advocating as I thought myself to be. As is often the case my rude awakening came in the midst of a real event.

It was Sunday morning in the family service at the National City Christian Church in Washington, D. C. I was presiding at the Lord's Supper after having given the invitation for all who love Jesus and wish to remember him to share in the Supper. Apparently I was taken at my word for my wife, Eleyce, offered the bread and the cup to our two small children who I am sure loved Jesus in a way that our Lord would have cherished. There she was right down front where all could see doing what Disciples of Christ and Christians of all persuasions just don't do. And what was my reaction? I quickly ran through the emotions of surprise, dismay, anger and embarrassment. To my shame my first thought was "What will people think?" My second thought was how could Eleyce place me in this difficult situation where I would have to explain and apologize for their behavior?

When the service was over I confronted her as quickly as possible with the question "Why? Why did you serve the Lord's Supper to our children?" Her response went straight to the heart of the matter, "Why not?" Somehow, "Because Disciples just don't commune children" wasn't an adequate answer to the question, "Why not?" She went on to say that she was explaining the Lord's Supper to them and echoing my invitation that we do this as a way of remembering Jesus and expressing our love to him to which my daughter said, "I remember Jesus," and my son said, "I love Jesus."

While it is true that Disciples rarely if ever communed unbaptized children prior to the mid-twentieth century, the prohibition was based on what was believed to be the tradition of the church since time immemorial. In this as in so many matters of faith and practice, the immediate past is viewed as the ancient tradition. In examining the child's place at the Lord's Table through time we can deepen our understanding of communion and gain spiritual strength in its practice and more nearly approximate our Lord's will as we gather around the table as a community of faith. Too often the decision to commune or not to commune children is simply a loss of memory, an accident of history, the reconstruction of our tradition for mundane reasons or the effort to push forward a theological position. Both "why?" and "why not?" are questions that the responsible Christian must always be willing to ask and to which he/she must be prepared to respond if our faith is to be the living, dynamic center of our lives that it is meant to be and our religious practices the valid expression of that faith.

So it was that I was pushed into the search for the answer to the question, *Why not?* Why are children, even baptized children in many traditions, excluded from participation in the Lord's Supper? This search has been primarily historical in character although this does not preclude biblical and theological considerations because these three approaches, historical, biblical and theological, cannot be separated without doing violence to each. It must of necessity also include educational, psychological and ecclesiastical considerations for all of these things come to a focus in the life of the individual child who either participates or does not participate in the Lord's Supper.

We will look at the development of the role of the child in the observance of the Lord's Supper through time from the birth of the church to the present. Because the Lord's Supper is the principal rite of community of the Christian Church and because the Christian Church (Disciples of Christ) has reaffirmed its centrality, the child's relationship to this sacrament must be clarified if we are to understand the child's relationship to the life of the Church. The Lord's Supper is thus the pivotal issue of our concern if the child is to share significantly in the life of the worshipping community.

For those who wish to know where this journey will lead us let me begin with the conclusion to which I have been led. While there may be some ecclesiastical reasons for excluding children from the Lord's Supper, there are no scriptural or theological reasons for doing so. Ecclesiastically we have assumed a tradition of rather recent origin when placed against the 2,000-year history of the Church. The fascinating history of children's participation in the Lord's Supper can be summarized in a few words: By the beginning of the Protestant Reformation in the 16th Century we find that children's communion had been the general practice of the Western Church for at least two-thirds of its fifteen hundred year history and for at least a third of that time, and probably longer, children had communed with their parents and congregations as a general practice. The Eastern Church had always practiced children's communion from its earliest memory to the present time. We thus find that one-half of the Christian Church has always practiced children's communion and the other half practiced it for the first half of its 2,000-year history. It was due to the efforts of Thomas Aquinas (ca.1225-1274) that communion was taken away from children at the same time the cup was taken away from the laity. The developing doctrine of the Real Presence (transubstantiation) gave a fatal blow to children's communion that lingered on in some ancient and prestigious parishes and remote areas of Christendom awaiting the *coup de grace* dealt it by the Council of Trent (1545-1563). The gradual recovery of children's participation in the Lord's Supper began in the mid twentieth century and continues to this day in much of Western Christendom.

John T. Hinant
Fall, 2005

Acknowledgments

While there are many people to whom I am grateful for their advice, encouragement and help in the completion of this study, there are several to whom I am especially indebted and whom I wish to publicly acknowledge.

The late James Blair Miller, professor of Christian education at Christian Theological Seminary, modeled for me what it means to be a children's advocate and a church educator. He encouraged me in my interest and study of children and the Lord's Supper and provided invaluable guidance.

Keith Watkins, professor of worship at Christian Theological Seminary, while not always agreeing with my conclusions, recognized the importance of what I was trying to do and was the first to suggest that I publish my study.

Kaye Edwards, Director of Family and Children's Ministries of the Division of Homeland Ministries of the Christian Church (Disciples of Christ), who has the gift of seeing through the eyes of children and translating what she sees into programs for the whole church was persistent in seeing that I finished this project and offered opportunities through workshops to hear what the church is saying and to share with them what I believe.

Sharon Warner, professor of Christian education at Lexington Theological Seminary, whose abundant enthusiasm for children's ministry spilled over into support of this project helped to bring it into print.

I am deeply grateful to the 1,737 Disciple ministers and laypersons who responded to the questionnaire for their churches. Without their candor, their passion and their desire to communicate their beliefs, the study would have been little more than bloodless statistics.

Robert L. Friedly, editor emeritus of *DisciplesWorld*, read the manuscript and made valuable suggestions some of which were painful but invariably correct.

Eleyce, my wife, opened my eyes to the need for such a study and shared the journey with me providing encouragement, suggestions, help and long hours at the computer. Without her it would never have been begun or completed. Her firm but gentle hand is evident to the writer throughout the finished product and I am indebted to her more than I can say.

Contents

Children at the Lord's Table

Preface
Acknowledgments

Part I: Finding a Place at the Table

The Child's Life in the Cradle of Christianity	2
Children in the Church of the Apostles	4
Children in the Church Coming of Age	7
Children's Communion in a Favored Church	13
The Fourth Century	14
The Fifth Century	17
The Sixth Century	19
The Seventh Century	20
The Eighth Century	22
The Ninth Century	23
The Tenth Century	24
The Eleventh Century	26
The Twelfth Century	26
The Thirteenth Century	29
The Fourteenth Century	31
The Fifteenth Century	32
Children's Communion in a Divided Church	33
The Roman Catholic Tradition	34
The Anglican Tradition	36
The Lutheran Tradition	41
The Reformed Tradition	46
The Christian Church (Disciples of Christ)	49

Part II: There's Room at the Table

Report of 2000/2001 Survey of the Christian Church (Disciples of Christ) Concerning the Role of the Child in the Observance of the Lord's Supper	55
Statistical Summary	57
Narrative Summary	63
Where the Bible Speaks	65
Church Tradition and Doctrine	71
How Open Should the Table Be?	77
How Much Do We Need To Know To Participate?	90
Accommodating Our Diversity	99
Education for Communion	105
Unintended Consequence of the Survey	119
Continuum of Children's Communion Participation in the Christian Church (Disciples of Christ)	121
There's Room at the Table	123
Appendix 1 – Survey Form	129
Appendix 2 – Survey Statistics by State	130
Appendix 3 – Survey Statistics by Question	132
Source Notes	136

PART I

Finding a Place at the Table

*A History of
Children's Participation
in the Lord's Supper*

The Child's Life in the Cradle of Christianity

We begin our story in the cradle of Christianity, the Jewish community, where the Christian Church was given life by the Holy Spirit and in which it grew and was nurtured by a community of faith until it found its own maturity in Christ. The Jewish attitude toward children and their ritual participation at the beginning of the Christian era is, therefore, important to us for the light it sheds on what the attitude of Jesus and the Jewish Christians must have been for they all shared a common ethos. Jewish Christianity did not constitute a radical discontinuity with its Jewish precursor so we may look at the first century Jews and extrapolate from their practices an understanding of the behavior of Jewish Christians toward their children.

William Barclay reminds us that, "No nation has ever set the child in the midst more deliberately than the Jews did,"[1] so it is no wonder that Jesus would chide his disciples for not allowing the children to come to him. This child-centered attitude of Jewish culture is borne out by the high priority given the education of children and the prominence of teachers in Jewish society and the respect that they enjoyed. Jesus certainly shared this view as evidenced by his attitude toward children and the fact that he accepted the title, "Rabbi." Jewish education was at its zenith in New Testament times enjoying an "age of the widest literacy for eighteen hundred years to come."[2]

Jewish education was education in holiness, a practical kind of wisdom to enable one to know God and live successfully. A principal means of education in holiness was the participation of children in the ritual observances of the Jewish religion. The Jewish Feasts and Festivals were opportunities for instruction in history and the generosity of God.[3] It is interesting to note that religious education for the Jewish child was not instruction about ritual but participation in ritual, providing an action/reflection model of education. This is an important point to keep in mind as one considers the validity of a child's participation in the Lord's Supper, if rituals are a form of religious instruction as many believe them to be.

The Jews were neither embarrassed nor inconvenienced by the presence of children in the full religious life of the community. In fact, the Feasts' and Festivals of the Jews developed in such a way that children had an important role in their observance and these cultic practices enabled the child to experience, appropriate and understand the faith of the community of which he was a part.

Children in the Church of the Apostles

The attitude of Jesus toward children is made abundantly clear in the Gospel narrative. A picture emerges of one who is never too busy or too preoccupied to receive and welcome a child. Furthermore, Jesus reserved his harshest judgment for those who hindered the religious development of the child (Matthew 18:6; Luke 17:2; Mark 9:42). In light of the teaching of Jesus it may seem surprising to some, e.g., William Barclay,[1] to find so little guidance in the New Testament regarding the teaching and training of the child. In fact, there are only five specific instructions regarding the care and nurture of children in the entire New Testament: Ephesians 6:1; Colossians 3:21; I Timothy 3:4, 12; Titus 1:6; 2 Corinthians 12:14. Given the attitude of Jesus, however, it was more likely that little more need to be said.

The Early Church did not constitute an abrupt break with its Jewish predecessor and much of what was important to the Jews continued into and became a part of the Christian community. Religious education for the Jewish child began in the fourth year.[2] We, can, therefore, use the silence of the early Jewish Christian communities about children and the Lord's Supper as an argument for the retention of the prevailing practice. In the same way that it is not necessary to instruct a skilled carpenter in the use of his hammer or an experienced cook in the making of bread so it was not necessary to instruct these new Christians, especially the Jewish Christians, in the education of their children for they already knew what was required of them and how they were to do it. Silence regarding an important matter is an argument for the *status quo*. In the same way one can assume that in the absence of advice or information to the contrary the prevailing custom regarding participation in ritual observances would be the norm. Lietzman and Schaff, important historians of the early church, both remind us that the members of the earliest church were Jews and wished to remain so.[3]

One must recognize, however, that the foregoing argument would not hold for Gentile Christians whose relation to Jewish culture bordered on rejection. This underscores the difficulty of discovering a normative pattern of church life in the New Testament that has been the goal of the Restoration Movement within the Christian Churches. We are reminded by scholars such as W. D. Davies in his book, *Christian Origins and Judaism*, that "the Church in the New Testament can assume many forms, and is not limited to any one form which is peculiarly the expression of its very being."[4]

The success of Paul's mission to the Gentiles and the struggle of the Jewish Christians to retain their identity within a hostile community had the inevitable consequence of Gentile Christianity eclipsing the power and authority of the original Christian community. Lietzmann puts it in stark language: "The fate of Jewish Christianity was "everywhere that of a quiet death in isolation. The church of the new victorious world-wide Christianity, which was now waxing mightily, took no note of the death of her elder sister."[5] This death is described by Lietzmann:

> The original church disappeared with the migration to Pella and the destruction of Jerusalem. At the same time it sank below the horizon of Gentile Christianity which was in process of conquering the world and which had thereby become dominant in Christendom....It [Jewish Christianity] sank to oblivion in the lonely deserts of East Jordan. In later centuries Christian theologians only occasionally cast curious eyes at these remnants of a most honourable past, and told their own contemporaries about them as a strange phenomenon. In the catalogue of theological terms these Jewish Christians are set down under the rubric of "heretics," but only very few people can ever have bothered themselves about these inhabitants of a remote region."[6]

It would have been in the Jewish Christian Church that the role of the child would have been elaborated in its ritual practices and a model for succeeding generations would have been provided. The oblivion of this branch of the Church took with it whatever might have been definitely known about the child's participation in the Lord's Supper in the Apostolic Age. Flying lower than the radar of theological inquiry the role of the child in the observance of the Lord's Supper escapes our scrutiny. However, it is not too much to believe that the Jewish Apostles brought with them into Jewish Christianity and then into Gentile Christianity the same attitude, understanding and practices regarding children into which they were born and which was a part of their memory from their own childhood.

✢ ✢ ✢

Children in the Church Coming of Age

The 225 years between the death of the Apostle John and the calling of the Council of Nicea in 325 CE, the first great ecumenical council, was an age of persecution and martyrdom. During this time the church grew stronger and expanded rapidly. It was a time of tremendous energy in which the church established itself and became the dominant faith in the Mediterranean world. It was a time in which there was great conflict between those who considered themselves to be defenders of the faith culminating in the Council of Nicea in 325 CE that articulated the faith of the Christian Church in the Nicene Creed. One is struck, however, by the infrequent references to children and their role in the life of the church. Earlier we could say that they were probably included if they weren't expressly excluded from the Lord's Supper. This position, however, becomes less viable the farther one is removed from the Jewish Christian Church and more documentary proof is required to support their inclusion.

There are at least four explicit references to the inclusion of children in the Lord's Supper during this period and no documents that would suggest their exclusion during this two-century span of which the writer is aware. The earliest reference is that of the *Canons of the Church of Alexandria* variously dated from the end of the second century to the early part of the third century. The canon is cautionary regarding the behavior of children (boys) at the Lord's Supper. The very casualness with which boys are mentioned enhances its value as reflecting what was in no way unusual or even worthy of note:

> Canon Twenty-ninth. Of the keeping of oblations which are laid upon the altar, —that nothing fall into the sacred chalice, and that nothing fall from the priests, nor from the boys when they take communion; that an evil spirit rule them not, and that no one speak in the protection (sanctuary), except in prayer; and when the oblations of the people cease, let psalms be read with all attention, even to the signal of the bell; and of the sign of the cross, and the casting of the dust of the altar into the pool."[1]

The second explicit reference to children's participation in the Lord's Supper is the interesting experience reported by Cyprian in *de Lapsis* that we shall quote in full:

> I will tell you what happened in my own presence. The parents of a certain little girl, running out of town in a fright had forgot to take any care of their child, whom they had left in the keeping of a nurse. The nurse had carried her to the magistrates: they, because she was too little to eat the flesh, gave her to eat before the idol some of the bread mixed with wine, which had been left of the sacrifice of those wretches. Since that time

her mother took her home. But she was no more capable of declaring and telling the crime committed, than she had been before of understanding or of hindering it. So it happened that once when I was administering, her mother, ignorant of what had been done, brought her along with her. But the girl being among the saints could not with any quietness hear the prayers said; but sometimes fell into weeping, and sometimes into convulsions, with the uneasiness of her mind: and her ignorant soul, as under a wrack, declared by such tokens as it could, the conscience of the fact in those tender years. And when the service was ended and the deacon went to give the cup to those who were present; and the others received it, and her turn came; the girl by a divine instinct turned away her face shut her mouth, and refused the cup. But yet the deacon persisted: and put into her mouth, though she refused it, some of the sacrament of the cup. Then followed reachings [retching] and vomiting. The eucharist could not stay in her polluted mouth and body; the drink consecrated in our Lord's blood burst out again from her defiled bowels....This happened in the case of an infant who was by reason of her age incapable of declaring the crime which another had acted on her.[2]

This incident, reported in the middle of the third century, leaves absolutely no doubt that this was not only a very young girl but also that she was not only permitted but even required to take communion!

Because of his stand on infant baptism, Cyprian was also left with a decision regarding communion. In a letter to Fidus who wanted to postpone baptism until the eighth day because newly born babies were so ugly and it would be distasteful to give them the kiss of peace as was customary following baptism, Cyprian advised Fidus that no delay should be allowed because "the mercy and grace of God is not to be refused to any one born of man."[3] This affirmation of the infant's right of access to the means of grace together with Cyprian's account of administering communion to a young child establishes beyond any reasonable doubt the practice of child communion by the middle of the third century.

The third direct reference to child communion is found in the *Didascalia Apostolorum* [Teaching of the Apostles]. *The Didascalia* is universally recognized as a third century work though opinion differs whether it is to be assigned to the first or the second half of the century. The book has been classed as the third in point of time to that group of documents known as the Church Orders that also includes the *Didache* and the *Apostolic Tradition* of Hippolytus. The *Didascalia* is essentially an elementary treatise on pastoral theology. Its special interest for us is that it describes where people are to be standing, sitting or kneeling in the church during the Eucharist including the following instructions regarding children: "And let the children stand on one side, or let their fathers and mothers take them to them; and let them stand up. And let the young girls also sit apart; but if there is no room, let them stand up behind the women. [4]

The final reference is from the *Constitutions of the Holy Apostles, Book VIII*. There are various opinions regarding its date ranging from the apostolic age to the early fourth century. The liturgy is described in great detail and the participation of children is carefully delineated. During the bidding prayer for the catechumen, we find children are instructed to make the response, "Lord, have mercy upon him," for each catechumen followed by the rest of the people. Following the bidding prayers we find the children standing at the reading desk under the watchful eye of the deacon. [The writer finds this early precedent for the male members of the diaconate to care for children during the church service intriguing!] Later, when the catechumen and the unbelievers have been dismissed, the mothers receive their children and the liturgy continues. The order for receiving communion is prescribed, "Let the bishop partake, then the presbyters, and deacons, and sub-deacons, and the readers, and the singers, and the ascetics; and then of the women, the deaconesses, and the virgins, and the widows; then the children; and then all the people in order, with reverence and godly fear, without tumult." Not only are children given a specific responsibility in the service, a response to the bidding prayers for the catechumen, they are given preference in receiving communion over everyone else except certain special individuals and groups. [5]

These four passages, while few in number, are important documents from the Early Church and do establish the presence of children at communion possibly as early as the latter part of the second century and certainly no later than the middle of the third. The fact that the references were casual in their mention of children is a strong argument that the practice was an accepted custom that required no explanation or defense. In the case of Cyprian, the only reason the event was noted was that it served to illustrate the situation of lapsed Christians who sought to return to the church after the persecutions—not the fact that the communicant was a young girl.

From this time on communicating children became a common practice in the Roman Church until the thirteenth century and it continues in the Eastern Orthodox Church to this day. In a personal letter, John Meyendorf of St. Vladimir's Orthodox Seminary expressed surprise that I should even ask the position of the Greek Orthodox Church, "And since it has always been taken for granted that Baptism and Communion are theologically inseparable parts of Church membership, the principle of giving Communion to children was universally accepted together with infant Baptism."[6] Even as late as the Council of Trent in the mid-sixteenth century, the Roman Catholic Church in an attempt to discourage the practice would only go as far as to say that any who asserted that baptized children were obligated to commune were anathema [cursed and excommunicated].[7] In spite of a serious effort to discourage children's communion the council would only go as far as to say it wasn't necessary.

Children's Communion in a Favored Church

During the Fourth and Fifth Centuries the Church became the Church Triumphant as it witnessed the end of persecution and the collapse of the Ancient World with the Fall of Rome. During this time infant communion became universal with three of the greatest Church Fathers, Augustine, Jerome and Chrysostom declaring that the communion of infants was necessary for their salvation.

Part I · Finding a Place at the Table

The Fourth Century

By the beginning of the fourth century, the Church both East and West was prepared to withstand the shock of the last and most terrible of the persecutions under the Emperor Diocletian. Having despaired of forcing the Christians (including his wife and daughter who if not Christians were favorable to the Christian religion) to recant their faith, he turned over the reins of government to four co-regents and retired to his farm to raise cabbages. Galerius, one of the co-regents, intensified the persecution in 304 but saw that it was not working and issued an edict of toleration in 311 which allowed the Christians to hold their religious assemblies if they didn't disturb the state. Galerius believed the Christians should be grateful for this grace and pray *to their god* for the welfare of the state, the emperor and themselves.[1] A short time later in A.D. 313, Constantine the Great issued his own edict of toleration that moved from the hostile neutrality of Diocletian to a friendly neutrality and protection including the restoration of property.[2] The church seized the reins of authority and a close relationship between church and state evolved that did not cease until the Protestant Reformation. In this favorable environment the story continues.

The fourth century opened with the Church's concern for those who failed to pass the test of martyrdom. Canon 1 of the Synod of Elvira in Spain in the years 306/312 refused communion to adults who had offered sacrifices to idols during the persecutions even if they were on their deathbed. From the specific mention of adults one can conclude that this penalty did not apply to young children who were not yet responsible.[3] This exception demonstrates a certain generosity in terms of knowledge and intention.

In Sicily we find a tombstone inscription dated some time prior to 337 for a Juliana Florentina. The inscription tells us that Juliana died at the age of 18 months, 22 days after

14

receiving emergency baptism and communion at two in the morning and communion again at four.[4] It is interesting that she was baptized when she was 1½ and apparently only then because she was dying. This indicates that infant baptism was not yet universal although it was to become so during the time of Augustine (354-430) who was not baptized until the age of 33.[5] Gregory of Nazianzus (ca. 325-390 proposed baptism, and therefore first communion, when the child was at least three-years-old and had some rational understanding.[6] Both St. Ambrose (d. 397) and St. Optatus of Milevis (c. 365) seem to suggest that the consecrated elements left over from the eucharist (reserved sacrament) were to be used for infants following baptism as well as for the sick and the dying in their respective churches.[7]

An especially interesting account is that from the travel diary of the nun, Egeria, written during her visit to Jerusalem in 394. She reports her visit to a church and notes that the boys responded to the reading of the names of the persons to be commemorated with the *Kyrie eleison*. It can be reasonably assumed that they communed as well.[8]

Three Church Fathers whose lives spanned the last half of the fourth century and on into the fifth made important contributions to the development of infant communion. Jerome (342-420) recognized that baptism and confirmation were being separated not because of any change in theological understanding but simply because of the rapid spread of Christianity. This made it difficult for the bishops to visit their distant parishes with any regularity or frequency. The local priest or deacon baptized and communed the newly baptized, whether infant, child or adult, and the bishop confirmed them on his next visit. What later became a theological issue was simply a matter of geography perhaps aggravated by a shortage of bishops and, we can presume, the reluctance of bishops to make the long and arduous trips more often than absolutely necessary.[9]

Part I · Finding a Place at the Table

Chrysostom (347-407) spoke of bringing up children in the Divine word[10] and was apparently in no great hurry to bring children to repentance by fear for he advises parents to wait until a child is fifteen before letting him/her hear of hell.[11] The Divine word must have referred to the liturgy and the obligations of parents to share in it with their children.

Augustine (354-430) referred to John 6:33 to support a belief that communion was necessary for everyone: "So Jesus said to them, 'Truly, truly, I say to you, unless you eat the flesh of the Son of man and drink his blood, you have no life in you.'"[12] Remarking on this passage, he says, in *Sermon 174, Sec. 7*, "They are infants; but they are made partakers of his table, that they may have life in themselves."[13] It is curious, however, that in his writings stressing the necessity of communion for the newborn, nothing suggests that communion was repeated during infancy or early childhood.[14]

The triumph of the church in the fourth century transformed the domestic spirit of worship found in the house-churches of an earlier time in which everyone participated, including children, into the public worship of the great basilicas of the fourth century in which nominal Christians shared the Lord's Supper with decreasing frequency. This reached its lowest point in the seventh century resulting in a rule laid down in the ninth century requiring lay people, including children, to take communion at least once a year at Easter.[15]

The Fifth Century

As we enter the fifth century we find the theological scene dominated by Jerome, Chrysostom and Augustine whose views on baptism and communion prevailed. The Lord's Supper was not a subject of theological controversy.[16] Even Pelagius, whose controversy with Augustine over the doctrine of original sin enlivened the fifth century, did not question infant baptism in spite of his opposition to the doctrine of original sin[17] and was consequently favorable to infant communion.

Pope Innocent 1, sitting on the papal throne from 401 to 417, reaffirmed the necessity of communion for young children[18] and reiterated the principle that the confirmation of infants was the proper function of no one other than the bishop.[19] The problem this created was that although local priests could administer communion to children as theologically required, they could not do so if the child had not been confirmed by the bishop whose visits might be few and far between.

In the Greek and Oriental Churches the custom of communing children apart from baptism continued until 1850: "Even infants, from the very time of their baptism, partake as often as their parents desire it."[20] The practice is still recognized by Gennadius of Marseilles in 495 in the West although the practice is beginning to fall away: "If they are infants... let those who bring them answer for them, according to the custom of baptism, and so, confirmed by the Laying on of Hands and the Chrism, let them be admitted to the mysteries of the Eucharist."[21]

Part I · Finding a Place at the Table

As alien hordes swept across Europe, a darkness descended upon the land that was to last five centuries. The Church with its spiritual strength and newfound secular power went forth to transform these people into Christians with both persuasion and coercion. The faith of the church and its sacraments of grace had to be proclaimed, explained and interpreted again and again with the inevitable changes that accompany such a task. **The Church sought to retain its ancient traditions, among them the communion of infants and children.** *Attention was focused primarily on how the wine was to be given (spoons, straws, leaves, fingers, etc.), the age of the communicant, the frequency of communion and the sequence of communion and confirmation.*

The Sixth Century

The first five centuries of the Middle Ages, the period from C.E. 476 to the end of the 10th century which we commonly call the Dark Ages, saw little significant development in the practice of infant/child communion. After the fall of the Roman Empire the so-called Dark Ages saw the rapid expansion of Christianity into Northern Europe. The conquerors from the North came to Rome for plunder and returned home with Christianity. During this time the church was expanding rapidly into Northern Europe, consolidating its gains and bringing religious order and stability to a chaotic situation.

Most of the literature from this time having to do with children's communion is found in the proceedings of church councils and the canons they legislated and the actions of bishops. These deal primarily with the mode and frequency of infant/child communion, the age of the communicant and the frequency of communion. We shall look at some representative samplings of these actions for the light they shed on our story.

Pseudo-Dionysius, possibly of the fifth but more likely of the sixth century, says, "Children who cannot understand divine things are yet made partakers of divine generation, and of the divine communion of the most sacred mysteries." [22.] The *Gelasian Sacramentary* of the sixth century, named for Gelasius who was Pope from 492 to 496, provided for infant communion but doesn't seem to contemplate the use of wine alone that became the custom,[23] because the young might choke on the bread and defile it by expelling it.

Evagrius, who completed his history in 594, demonstrates the continuing of children's communion when he mentions an "ancient custom" at Constantinople: "When there remained a good quantity of the holy portions of the undefiled body of Christ our God, uncorrupted boys from among those who attended the school of an undermaster were sent to consume them."[24] In France, "almost the same thing was practiced, but with a little more ceremony, according to the Decree of the Second Council of Mascon, assembled in the year 585."[25]

In 593 Pope Gregory I wrote a letter to Januarius, Bishop of Sardinia, in which he said, "Priests are not to presume to sign infants on the forehead with sacred chrism; but priests may administer chrism on the breast, that bishops may afterwards administer it on the forehead."[26] This would have been followed with communion.

The Seventh Century

Early in the 7th Century, the *Gregorian Sacramentary* provided for infant communion but didn't seem to contemplate the use of wine alone.[27] The most ancient copy of this document contains the direction that if the Bishop is present the infant shall be confirmed immediately following baptism and shall "after that communicate; and if the Bishop is not there, shall be communicated by the Presbyter."[28]

St. Austin was sent to England in 597 by Pope Gregory I where he died in 604. He strongly affirmed the necessity of infant communion on several occasions including this:

> Let us hear the Lord saying of the Sacrament of the Holy Table, unto which no body approaches as they ought, unless they are first Baptized; "If ye eat not my Flesh, and drink not of my Blood, you have no Life in you." What more do we look for, what can be replied to this, only that obstinacy knits its Sinews to resist the Force of this evident truth? Else durst any one deny, but that this Speech concerns little Children, and that they can have life in themselves, with the participation of this Body and of this Blood?...It is with great reason that the Christians of Africa call Baptism, Salvation,

and the Sacrament of the Body of Christ, Life; whence is that, as I think, but from an ancient and Apostolical Tradition, by which the Churches of Christ hold for certain, That no body can attain, either unto the Kingdom of God, or unto Salvation or eternal Life, without the Kingdom of God, or unto Salvation or eternal Life, without Baptism and the participation of the Supper of our Lord. [29]

Gregory the Great sent Paulinus to England as a papal missionary in 601 where he lived until his death in 644. Paulinus emphasized the necessity of infant communion. It was preferable to do this after confirmation but if necessary it could be done before confirmation.

As a parenthical note since our attention has shifted from the Eastern Church where the changes in children's communion are not as great, it can be mentioned that John Moschus tells the story in 630 of some children who imitated the celebration of the Eucharist "as they had witnessed and taken part in it themselves." [30] This affirms the continuing incidence of children's communion as contrasted with a one-time communion of infants at the time of baptism which soon became the norm in the Western Church.

Some time during the 7th Cenury the Church of Portugal introduced the practice of giving infants the consecrated Bread sopped in Wine, for which a spoon was generally used. This practice was soon adopted in the Greek Church but was just as quickly forbidden in the West. [31]

A canon of the Council of Toledo in 675 commands communicating infants immediately after baptism. [32] Canon xi of the same council does not intend the actual use of the wine alone but the use of an accompanying drink from the chalice for the purpose of swallowing the bread. This leads to communicating with only the wine for those who can't swallow the bread such as children and the sick. This method would also commend itself to those places where intinction was disapproved because of its association with Judas who received the sopped bread.[33]

The Eighth Century

The Venerable Bede's concern for children's communion in England is poignantly expressed in a letter written in 734 when he believed himself dying:

> And yet there are innumerable boys and girls, young men and maidens, old men and women, of most chaste life, who, beyond all doubt or controversy, might be allowed to communicate in the heavenly mysteries every Sunday, and also on the feasts of the apostles and martyrs, as you yourself have seen them do in the Holy Roman and Apostolic Church.[34]

The Council of Clofesho apparently responded to the Venerable Bede's concern for it admonished the young to communicate often.[35] As the council expressed it, "Youths of the laity, not yet corrupted by the temptations to which their age is prone, are to be exhorted often to communicate."[36]

Toward the end of the eighth century general changes began to take place. *Codex Juris Canonical* in 788 seems to be pivotal in several respects for it ordered that confirmation be delayed no longer than the seventh year because it is a part of baptism and *must* be completed before first communion. This reaffirmed confirmation as a part of baptism and put first communion no later than seven but the earlier the better.[37]

In the most ancient *Ordo Romanus*, a Directory of Ritual, probably of the eighth century, infant baptism on Easter Eve is ordered with care that the infants "take no food nor be suckled before they partake of the Sacraments of the Body of Christ," which they did daily during Easter Week.[38] In what may have been a later edition of the *Ordo Romanus*, the decree takes on a relaxed form: "Care is to be taken that young Children receive no Food after they are Baptized, and that they should not give them Suck without great necessity, until they have participated in the Body of Christ."[39]

In Eastern Christendom the eighth century Barberini *Euchologion* orders the communion of infants following the baptismal service. In the modern text, however, ablution and the cutting of hair takes place eight days after the baptism but communion is not apparently required.[40]

Specific instances of infant communion *in extremis* (last rites) from the beginning of the eighth century are to be found.[41] And in a treatise written by the order of Charlmagne (747-814) and in his name, he refers to the communion of infants and, in his *Capitularies*, he commands that priests be ready to communicate the sick "be they young or old.[42]

The Ninth Century

Very little is added to the development of infant/child communion in the ninth century or to our understanding. It is briefly mentioned in the third Council of Tours in 813[43] Bishop Jesse of Amiens (d. 836) sought to justify the baptismal rite in the Easter Vigil:

> Finally (that is, after baptism and confirmation) the baby is strengthened with the blood of Christ. So he becomes a member of Him who died for him and has risen, as the Lord has said Himself: 'Who eats my flesh….' Just as our body cannot live without soul, likewise only the one who is strengthened with the Body of Christ has the spirit of life. Consequently he who wants to live, let him draw near, let him believe that he lives from God, that is incorporated in God in order to vivified."[44]

Raban Maur, an Englishman who lived from 776 to 856, speaks of communion after baptism but makes no mention of confirmation.[45] Gautier, Bishop of Orleans in 869, and Riculfe, Bishop of Soissons in 889, spoke of the necessity of communing infants in danger of death.[46] And Theodulf, another ninth century bishop of Orleans, tells us that "the church has received from the Lord Himself the custom of nourishing with His Body all those who are reborn from water and the Spirit; for, as He said, only by force of this food can one remain in Christ and He in him and attain, like Elias, the top of the mountain which is Christ."[47]

The Tenth Century

From the laws of Howel the Good, drawn up in 926, we have evidence of confession as a way of examining oneself prior to communion at an early age in Wales. "From every person who has been baptized,' states the code, "the bridaw (to affirm solemnly) may be taken, as well man as woman... from the child of the age of seven years, which shall go under the hand of the confessor."[48]

Aelfric (ca.955-1020) reaffirms the necessity of infant communion in England: "Ye should give the Eucharist to children when they are baptized, and let them be brought to mass that they may receive it all seven days that they are unwashed."[49] And in a pontifical from the church of Sens in France ca. 980 we find communion prescribed and confirmation following baptism is the bishop is present.[50]

A new millennium brought with it a division of Christendom into Eastern Orthodoxy and Western Catholicity. The Eastern Church continued its practice of infant communion unabated, but the Western Church entered a period of theological reappraisal due in large part to the developing doctrine of **the real presence** *of Christ in the communion elements making the communion of infants and children an issue. Thomas Aquinas rode the crest of this theological revolution that carried the church into the Renaissance and the end of the Middle Ages that withdrew the cup from the laity, leaving adults the bread and young children nothing, for the general practice was to commune infants and young children with the wine alone, due to the theological risk of choking on the bread, regurgitating it and thus profaning the body of Christ. During these five centuries, the principal task was to revise ecclesiastical history to show that communion for infants and children was not necessary and to determine when children should receive their first communion and under what circumstances.*

Part I · Finding a Place at the Table

The Eleventh Century

In the eleventh century we begin to see some backing off from earlier positions due to a changing theological climate. An example of this is the concern over persons who could not swallow such as infants due to the developing doctrine of the Real Presence. The reasoning was that if children were to choke on the bread and spit it up, then the body of Christ which had become the real presence of Christ in the bread would be profaned. This issue had apparently raised doubts in the mind of Domnaldus, an Irish bishop, whether infants were proper subjects to receive communion at all. Lanfranc, Archbishop of Canterbury opposed this view and stated in a letter to Domnaldus that persons of every age needed to fortify themselves by receiving the Lord's body and blood. [51] The Council of Clernon in 1098 forbade communion by intinction in its 28th canon thus making it more difficult to commune infants. [52]

The Twelfth Century

The doctrine of the Real Presence dominated the theological understanding and practice of the Lord's Supper in the Western Church during the twelfth century. Much of the discussion revolved about children's participation in the Lord's Supper. While much of the theological discussion of the time will sound alien to the modern mind, it did bring about profound changes in the church's attitude toward children's participation in the Lord's Supper. Restraints such as making age a requirement for communion came into place and are still followed in many of our churches although the doctrine of the Real Presence which gave them validity has long since been abandoned. And whatever else can be said, the medieval church was not unmindful of the presence of children and sought to accommodate them in the observance of the Lord's Supper in ways that would nurture their souls and insure their salvation. The modern church including the Disciples could learn much from their passion for children however misguided we believe their theology of the Lord's Supper may have been.

Communion *sub species sanguinus* [using wine only] was the principal emphasis of the communion of infants in the twelfth century. Radulphus Ardens of Poietiers at the beginning of the twelfth century reported, "It has been decreed that it (the Viaticum or communion given to a dying person) be delivered to children as soon as baptized, at least in the species of wine, that they may not depart without a necessary sacrament."[53] Pope Paschall II who died in 1118, wrote a letter to the abbot of Cluny in which he said that although Jesus, whose example we should follow, gave both bread and wine. In the case of infants and the sick who cannot swallow bread communion with only the wine is permissible.[54] This developing doctrine of concomitance was enunciated unequivocally by William of Champeaux, a scholastic theologian who died in 1121: "...to little children just baptized only the chalice is given, because they cannot assimilate bread, and in the chalice they receive Christ entire."[55]

In England the necessity of infant communion was reaffirmed, e.g., Gilbert, Bishop of Limerick from 1110 to 1139 reminded his priests that they must commune those who have just been baptized.[56] An anonymous English writer of this period articulated an intellectual requirement for communion: "Give not the Lord's Body to boys under ten years old, for though they are pure yet they know not what they receive. But if death is imminent, communion may be given them, though they are only nine, or eight, or even seven years old, if they know the Our Father and are good."[57] He also suggests the age of reason to be seven or later.

Hugh of St. Victor, a Frenchman who died in 1141, suggested that communion should be given to the newborn in the species of blood with the finger because they naturally suck.[58] He also voiced opposition to the custom of giving unconsecrated wine to infants and would have abandoned the practice if it wouldn't scandalize people.[59]

Others including Robert Pulleyn[60], a contemporary of Hugh St. Victor; Radulphus Ardens; Bernard of Sainter (1141-1166);[61] the School of Anselm of Leon (d. 1117) all agreed that communion is necessary to eternal life and the latter went so far as to say, "Once it has been received another reception of the sacrament can be deferred for a long time. But if children depart this life without the communion of Christ's body and blood, for the ministers there is negligence and peril, for the children there is not perdition."[62]

A Roman Pontifical of the twelfth century with a modification of *Ordo* suggests a unity of the three rites, baptism, confirmation and communion. It required that after baptism and confirmation by the pope, infant candidates are not to be fed, except for great necessity, before they receive the sacrament of the body of Christ.[63] Another Roman Pontifical of the same period addresses the difficulty of communing infants who can neither eat nor drink. It directs the presbyter to communicate them with a leaf or by placing in their mouths the presbyter's finger that he has dipped in the consecrated wine.[64]

Bishop Odo of Paris in 1193 prohibited the giving of communion to infants under any circumstances[65], and in 1197 the Archbishop of Paris prohibited the host being given to children before consecration.[66] By the end of the twelfth century, the Western Church had set in motion the theological and ecclesiastical actions that would withdraw communion from infants and young children. From this period on the church was increasingly reluctant to commune children but unable to totally deny it.

The Thirteenth Century

At the beginning of the thirteenth century it was becoming increasingly common to commune the laity with bread only so it was inevitable that the custom of communing infants with the wine only came into conflict. Since the church was reluctant to give the wine to the laity and was equally reluctant to give infants the bread it is not surprising that the communing of infants began to die out. This is borne out by the fact the Fourth Council of the Lateran meeting in 1215 made no mention of communicating children below the age of discretion.[67] Not only was infant communion dying out but in some places it was even prohibited as in Paris. In 1220 a boy of youthful piety, not quite seven, was dying and asked to partake of the holy eucharist but was denied because of the laws of the church! The Council of Treves in 1227 did prohibit the giving of communion to infants.[68] This was echoed two years later in France at the Council of Toulouse which also prohibited children's communion before the age of discretion.[69]

Little is being said about confirmation during this period that suggests that it is becoming less important in itself and in its relation to the Lord's Supper. The confusion about confirmation is exemplified by Alexander of Hales (d. 1245) who said that confirmation was invented by the Council of Meaux in 845.[70] Henry, bishop of Sisteron in England from 1240 to 1250 established several criteria for communion including seven years of age or older, confession and the learning of the Pater Noster [The Lord's Prayer]. He doesn't even mention confirmation.[71] The Council of Albi in 1254 denied communion to children before the *years of discretion* but didn't define the age at which it came.[72] In an English synod in 1255 it was prescribed that on Easter the Eucharist not be given to children, but only the blessed bread.[73]

It was Thomas Aquinas (ca. 1225-1274) who gave theological and ecclesiastical clout to the developing trend of denying communion to children. He was appointed by Pope Urban IV to write a liturgical service to be used on Corpus Christi. Two important changes were made by Thomas: the abandonment of the communion of children and the withdrawal of the cup from the laity.[74] The communion of children *in extremis* [near death] was also withdrawn in Aquinas' *"Supplement"* to his *"Theology"* in which he says that extreme unction and the eucharist were not administered to children because both sacraments required real devotion in the recipients.[75]

The Council of Cologne in 1280 ordered confirmation candidates of ten years or more to make their confession.[76] This implied that children under ten were not to be confirmed and assumes the *years of discretion* to be reached by ten; although a different reading of the proceedings suggests that the council established the age of seven as the age at which children were to be admitted to confirmation![74] At any rate the practice of deferring confirmation and thus communion to an age of reason was firmly established as the norm if not the practice by this time. Apparently some were communing children before confirmation making it necessary for Archbishop Peckham of Canterbury to decree in 1281 that no one could "make their communion" until they were confirmed.[78]

This understanding continued to spread. In Belgium in 1287 the Statutes of John of Liege prohibited the giving of communion to infants. They also established the *years of discretion* at ten years or older.[79] And in the *Synodal Statutes* of Cahors, Rodes and Tulli in France children were not to be communicated before the *age of discretion*,[80] but again this phrase was not defined.

The withdrawal of communion from infants and children was not, however, universal. Some time during the thirteenth century William of Auxerre in France said that infants should receive the body of Christ.[81] A thirteenth century manuscript of the *Ambrosian Manual* in Milan, Italy commands infant communion after baptism for the preservation of the soul. It describes the communion of infants by intinction [bread dipped in wine]. The infant was thus given both the bread and the wine. This practice continued in Milan until the end of the fifteenth century.

The Fourteenth Century

During the fourteenth century Western bishops continued issuing pontificals withdrawing communion from children and proposing that they wait until the *age of discretion* often without defining its meaning. In 1300 the Council of Bayeux in France permitted children seven years or over to commune.[82] And the Council of Constance in Germany required persons fourteen years or over to make their confession before being confirmed.[83] The Council of Avignon in 1227 prohibited children from receiving communion before the *age of discretion* without defining its meaning and the Council of Beziers took the same action in 1351.[84]

Remnants of the earlier practice, giving communion to newly baptized infants, persisted as attested by two pontificals, one in England and one in France. At some time during the fourteenth century an English bishop, Lacy, issued a pontifical in which he curiously writes that in the service for infant baptism, if a bishop is present the newly baptized must be immediately confirmed and then given communion "if he has the proper age."[85] This may refer to children and adults because the communion is given with bread. A pontifical of the Church of Amiens in France indicates that the church continued giving communion to infants [86] and was still doing it, although with common wine, in 1524 [87] and 1541.[88] Such instances are exceptions and represent "churches no doubt jealous of their ancient traditions, and sufficiently eminent to be able to maintain them in spite of what was happening elsewhere.[89]

The Fifteenth Century

On the eve of the Protestant Reformation infant and young children's communion ceased being observed in all except a few places, and the *age of discretion* without definition in most cases was the threshold for children's communion. To this withdrawal of communion from infants and children, the Greek theologian Simeon of Saloniki (d. 1429) representing the Eastern Church responds: "One objects that babies do not know what they receive (and hence reason prohibits us from admitting them to Holy Communion). What a silly objection! Why then do you baptize them and sign them with holy chrism?"[90] But the movement away from infant communion continued in the West and the Council of Cologne, feeling the uneasiness in 1457, indicated that many doubted the legality of confirming infants and required that the proper bishop give his consent if it was to be done.[91]

Children's Communion in a Divided Church

By the beginning of the Protestant Reformation in the sixteenth century we find that infant communion had been the general practice of the Western Church for at least two-thirds of its fifteen hundred year history and for at least a third of that time, and probably longer, children had communed with their parents and congregations as a general practice. In fact, there was a time when more children would commune than adults on any given Sunday because of the adult fear of partaking unworthily which would not be a concern for children because of their innocence.

The Protestant Reformation announced by Martin Luther in 1517 on the door of the Wittenberg church and the Counter Reformation by the Roman Catholic Church begun at the Council of Trent (1545-1563) in an effort to reform itself brought changes in the participation of children in the

Lord's Supper in Western Christendom reflecting the changing theological climate and the scrutiny accompanying it. Following the Protestant Reformation, the development of infant/child communion was stamped with the liturgical, theological and pastoral characteristics of the faith community in which it occurred.

We will first look at the development of children's communion in the Roman Catholic, Anglican, Lutheran and Reformed traditions. All of these practice infant baptism so their situations have some similarities that have been addressed in a variety of ways. We will then look at the Christian Church (Disciples of Christ) as representative of those churches practicing *believers* or *adult* baptism and the ongoing changes that began in the mid-twentieth century [with such children as my own participating in the Lord's Supper] and is continuing today in the Christian Church (Disciples of Christ). We will not continue the history of children's communion in the Eastern Orthodox Church because few major changes in the communing of children took place following the division of the Eastern and Western Churches begun in the ninth century culminating in the Great Schism of 1054.

The Roman Catholic Tradition

When the Council of Trent convened in the middle of the sixteenth century to put its theological/ecclesiastical house in order to meet the challenge of the Reformation it was faced with lingering traces of infant communion in spite of a three-hundred-year effort to abolish it. The Council was unwilling to put itself in the position of outright condemnation of infant communion considering the fact that it had such a long tradition and significant support from the Church Fathers. The Council, therefore, approached the issue in an oblique manner during Session XII (1652) by declaring anyone anathema [cursed] who claimed communion was necessary for small children.[1] Trivializing infant and young children's communion had the effect of banning it while not going so far as condemning it. In spite of the obvious discouragement of infant/child communion by the Roman Catholic Church the practice lingered on here and there and even today in some parts of Mexico and Latin American, children and even infants are confirmed immediately after Baptism and admitted to the Holy Communion."[2]

During the latter part of the thirteenth century, church councils had begun to reflect the sacramental theology of St. Thomas Aquinas and were suggesting the deferring of confirmation and communion to the "age of discretion" or "age of reason" as it was sometimes called. This "age of discretion"" was variously described, usually seven or ten, but never defined. Pope Pius X, in his *Quam Singulari* of August 8, 1910 decreed that a child should be admitted to first communion when he/she knew the difference between the Eucharist as a sacred meal and the family meal.[3] This is generally interpreted as seven.

While confirmation traditionally preceded first communion as the second part of the three-fold initiatory rite (baptism, confirmation, communion) in the Roman Catholic Church, the necessity of confirmation by a bishop sometimes postponed confirmation long after first communion. This exception became the general practice in a number of places such as the United States in spite of papal desires and canon law. For example, Pope Leo, in a letter to the Bishop of Marseilles, dated June 22, 1897, reaffirmed that first communion should occur after confirmation, a custom, however, that was restricted to isolated dioceses. The letter was prompted by the fact that it had become common to delay confirmation to the age of twelve or fourteen with first communion considerably earlier.[4] The argument for reversing the order was that young Christians need the "strength from heaven" available in communion if their physical and psychological maturation was to be achieved in harmony and grace."[5] Bonifaas Luykx also reminds us that confirmation after first communion is a recent innovation although it was practiced as a frequent exception at an earlier time when bishops were not always available to confirm and communion was necessary even for infants. In spite of theological opinion to the contrary, the American custom of first communion followed by confirmation about three years later has prevailed and is generally practiced by Catholics everywhere.

And when should children receive their first communion? Francis Buckley speaks for Roman Catholics in his book, "Children and God": The decision when a child is to take his first communion is not up to the parish priest but is a prerogative of the parents and the child. The priest is only an advisor because first communion is an event growing out of the family life and its particular style. This is why no arbitrary age should be set although what others do will no doubt influence parents and children in the parish.[6]

The Anglican Tradition

An understanding of children's communion in the Anglican tradition might well begin with the remarkable statement by Urban T. Holmes, III in 1972:

> Anglican theologians have in the past stated, without any support other than nine hundred years of English tradition, that one has to be confirmed to be admitted to Communion. This is an issue of Christian initiation;

and as most of us know it is a unique claim of Anglicanism that we are now rapidly and happily surrendering with the admission of young unconfirmed children to Communion. Anglicanism has always stood with the 1500-year tradition of the universal Church that one does not have to be confirmed "to be saved," but until now has certainly implied the opposite by requiring it for admission to Communion. In reversing our stand we have acknowledged something of what we no longer believe Confirmation to be in the course of becoming a member of the Church. What that "something" was remains a bit of a mystery, since in requiring Confirmation as the prerequisite for Communion no one had ever stated what made the laying on of hands by a bishop necessary. The argument tended to focus on pre-Confirmation instruction...and the need "to understand what we are doing." No one to my knowledge ever claimed that Confirmation itself imparted this enlightenment, that is, as doctrinal content or meaning, which is not what Justin Martyr meant in using the term of Baptism[7]

An understanding of the Anglican position must begin with John Peckham (c 1225-1292), Archbishop of Canterbury, who was sent to England with the papal instruction to enforce the Gregorian reforms in that frontier of the Christiana faith. One way in which Peckham sought to bring order and control to his uncivilized and independent people was to gain control over the bishops and through them to control their parishes by arbitrarily ruling that no one could participate in Holy Communion until he had been confirmed by a bishop. Holmes points out that this was without precedent and theologically impossible to defend.[8] One might add, however, that it was ecclesiastically effective!

Nearly three hundred years later, Thomas Cranmer (1489-1556), Archbishop of Canterbury, godfather of Princess Elizabeth, baptized her on September 10 just three days after her birth on September 7, 1533 and she was immediately confirmed.[9] This was either not recognized, ignored, or considered an exception due to her royalty because we know that at the same time English bishops were requiring an intellectual understanding of the faith for confirmation and confirmation was the prerequisite for communion. Thus in 1561 we find Bishop Parkhurst of Norwich refusing admittance to Holy Communion anyone who could not say the Lord's Prayer, Creed, and Ten Commandments.[10] This intellectual requirement will also be seen in the Lutheran meaning of confirmation as an entrance to communion and in the Reformed tradition whether called by the name confirmation or not. In 1565 Bishop Bentham of Lichfield required the clergy to present children at seven years of age.[11] Cox at Ely required that any one older than twenty who could not say the necessary forms by heart nor any between twelve and twenty who could not say the catechism be barred from communion.[12] This rather strict rule laid down between 1570 and 1574 was reiterated from place to place with only slight variation in age and requirement.[13] This particular rule for admission to the Lord's Supper did not imply that children under twelve who could say the catechism would not be admitted[14] but it did have that practical effect.

Cosin in his "Notes upon the Book of Common Prayer," written between 1619 and 1660, notes that infant confirmation, like infant communion, "is now taken away by the consent of the whole Western Church."[15] In 1662 the clause, "or be ready and desirous to be confirmed" was added to the Prayer Book following the statement, "And there shall none be admitted to the Holy Communion until such time as he be confirmed...." This was introduced to win the approval of the Presbyterian divines who had requested that "confirmation may not be made so necessary to the Holy Communion that none should be admitted unless they had been confirmed"[16]

In 1676 a Bishop of Norwich made the inevitable transition from sixteen as the age after which neglect of communion was an offense as specified by the Articles drawn up by order of Convocation in 1640 to sixteen as the age to begin to commune."[17] Ultimately, the strict examination for admission to communion resulted in its neglect and in 1714 we have John Johnson summing up the sad state to which participation in the Lord's Supper had fallen and his opinion of children's participation as follows:

> I am not ignorant, that many of the ancients did from hence conclude, and some Chrisian do to this day believe, that by virtue of this declaration of Jesus Christ (John 6:48-51) even infants are under an obligation of eating and drinking the Sacramental Body and Blood; but I must profess that I cannot see that this is fairly deducible from the words; for our Saviour speaks to grown persons, such as were capable of laboring or doing the work of God, that is, 'believing,' as He Himself explains it, to such as were capable for not believing, and therefore not to children; nor indeed was the communicating of children ever the universal practice of the Church; but I believe withal, that the giving the Sacramental Body and Blood to infants was a much more excusable practice than that contempt or neglect of it, which now so much prevails. God grant that what I have written may serve for the cure of this great evil.[18]

Apparently, as bad as communing children might be it was better than the lack of communing that was taking place in the English Church!

In 1853 Jeremy Taylor published his book, "The Worthy Communicant." It is an important book in the context of children's communion because it is fairly typical of much of the scholarly thought of the mid-nineteenth century and because it takes a neutral position making possible later developments: "It is certain," he writes, "that in Scripture there is nothing which directly forbids the giving [of] the Holy Communion to Infants....But as there is no prohibition of it, so no Command for it."[19] He later concludes that it is left to the discretion of the Church to commune or not to commune infants and children.[20] Taylor and other Anglican theologians of the same persuasion were laying the groundwork for action which would be taken a century later.

In 1939 the Bishop of Hull, Henry Vodden, privately circulated a document that proposed that children of ten or eleven years of age be prepared for Confirmation which would take place when they had reached "years of discretion" at the age of sixteen or more.[21] The Protestant Episcopal Church repudiated such efforts at reform in 1944 by reaffirming the earlier position hat no one may take Communion without being confirmed. But the effort continued and in January 1966 the Archdeacon of Rochdale, the Venerable L. G. Tyler, proposed to the Convocation of York that there be a study of the possibilities of experiments to separate admission to Holy Communion from Confirmation.[22] In his chapter of "Confirmation Crisis" published by the authority of the Executive Council of the Episcopal Church in 1968, J. D. C. Fisher sought to preserve the baptism/confirmation/communion rubric by confirming young children who were to be communed and adding a ratification of vows at a later date.[23] In "Prayer Book Study 18 of the Protestant Episcopal Church published in 1970 confirmation is seen as disrupting the connection between baptism and communion because of the delay it necessitates. Children, it maintains, should never be unable to remember making their communion. This suggests that first communion should be somewhere around three or four.[24] And finally in 1970 the House of Bishops of the Protestant Episcopal Church meeting in Houston voted to admit nonconfirmed baptized persons to communion thus changing the rubric, as far as children are concerned, to baptism/communion/confirmation! [25.]

The Lutheran Tradition

The principle criterion for participation in the Lord's Supper in the Lutheran Church for all Christians, young or old, has always been from Martin Luther to very recent times, an articulate understanding of one's faith and the meaning of the Lord's Supper. Instruction, which Lutherans have always associated with confirmation, has been the threshold over which Lutherans must step, the door already having been opened by baptism. The issue is, therefore, not specifically how old a child must be but how high the threshold must be to insure the proper participation in communion. It reminds one of the mark on a post at the entrance to a ride in an amusement park: If you're this tall you can ride.

Luther's concern was that Christians partake of the Lord's Supper in a worthy manner and this necessitated that everyone must first be asked to give an account of his faith, especially what he believed about the Lord's Supper and what he expected to receive from it. [26] This emphasis on instruction, especially in preparation for the Lord's Supper is, according to Repp, "Luther's major contribution to a new type of confirmation, for now it was to be associated not merely with Holy Baptism, as it had been in the past, but also with the Lord's Supper. [27] Luther's emphasis thus became the first step toward a new form of confirmation without actually establishing the rite.

This new kind of confirmation requiring intellectual understanding of the faith and an assent to it became a prerequisite to the Lord's Supper in the Lutheran tradition.

Part I · Finding a Place at the Table

It had nothing in common with confirmation in the early church or as it is found later in the Greek Orthodox and Roman Catholic Churches except the name. Its primary difference is in who initiates the act, God or the believer. The Christian Church (Disciples of Christ) has traditionally believed its own form of confirmation, confession of faith usually preceded by a pastor's class, is a prerequisite to share in the Lord's Supper. Because of the similarity of these requirements for participating in the Lord's Supper we will look more closely at the development of confirmation in the Lutheran tradition.

According to the analysis prepared by the Joint Commission on the Theology and Practice of Confirmation of the American Lutheran Church, the Lutheran Church in America, and The Lutheran Church—Missouri Synod published in 1967, there are six major emphases of confirmation resulting from the many influences and counter-influences which affect the practice of communion. They are the catechetical, the hierarchical, the sacramental, the traditional, the pietistic and the rationalistic.[28] The first four emphases are products of the sixteenth century and the latter two appeared in the seventeenth and eighteenth centuries.

The **catechetical** type of confirmation was simply a result of the need for instruction prior to communion and was not limited to those coming to their first communion. As such it was an unconscious prototype of confirmation and was the most common form of "confirmation" during the first one hundred and fifty years of the Lutheran Church. It is interesting to note that a parallel development occurred in the Reformed Church especially in Scotland which influenced the Disciples of Christ through the Campbells.

The **hierarchical** type of confirmation was introduced by Martin Bucer, a German theologian and associate of Luther, in 1538-1539. He added a subjective element when he introduced a vow in which the child pledged to surrender himself/herself to God and to submit himself to the discipline of the church.

The **sacramental** tendency was the laying on of hands which sometimes, but not always, suggested the actual imparting of the Holy Spirit. This gave confirmation a sacramental overtone that the Reformers had not intended but which continues to the present.

There was some effort to retain the **traditional** form without the Roman Catholic abuses. When this was done, first communion was postponed as much as one or two years and was clearly disassociated from the Lord's Supper. It emphasized the laying on of hands and the instruction that preceded it.

The **pietistic** form of confirmation appeared in the seventeenth century as a reaction to the decline in parish life in Germany resulting from the Thirty Years War, the French invasion and the Counter-Reformation. The confirmation vow became a renewal of the baptismal covenant and catechetical instruction and emphasized a "conversion" experience. The **rationalistic** type of confirmation was a reaction to the pietistic type. It was the event that stressed understanding and gave meaning to baptism.

A study document published in 1963 by the Commission on Education of the Lutheran World Federation states: "Confirmation is a rite which the Church has adopted in a free and responsible decision so that she may lead her young members to the right use of the Word and Sacrament and to a full life in the Christian congregation."[29] In the previously mentioned study document published by the Joint Commission on the Theology and Practice of Confirmation, confirmation is simply defined: "Confirmation is a pastoral and educational ministry of the church that is designed to help baptized children identify with the life and mission of the adult Christian community and that is celebrated in a public rite.[30]

Let us now return to the matter of when a child should have his/her first communion according to Lutheran practice. One cannot generalize regarding sixteenth century practice relative to the age for confirmation and first communion because there was such a wide diversity. The major criterion was the catechumen's readiness to participate and almost invariably the church orders used an expression such as "when the children come of age." According to German law, a child came of age when he reached twelve and according to Roman canon law it could be any age from seven to twelve.[31] At any rate, admission to first communion was much earlier than subsequent practice.

In America, the age for first communion tended to be older than in Europe. Benjamin Kurtz reported in 1843 that the majority of those confirmed in the United States were between fifteen and twenty years old.[32] By this time confirmation and first communion had once more been associated. It was not long before the age of thirteen or fourteen became the norm with fourteen being the most common to coincide with the completion of grammar school and entry into the adult world.[33]

Three schools of thought in Germany have debated the issue of confirmation and first communion. The conservative group contends that there should be no major change except for a moderation of the vow. First communion would follow confirmation. The liberal group suggests confirmation in several steps: early communion between eight and twelve following brief instruction on the Lord's Supper; a ritual to coincide with the completion of grammar school and the close of the baptismal instruction; and at about the age of eighteen an acceptance of the youth into the congregation and the granting of majority rights. A radical group proposes the abolition of confirmation. Children would be permitted to simply go to their first communion with their parents at any age and without ceremony except for the pastor's questioning of the children to avoid any abuses. One year after completion of grammar school the child would be examined by the pastor and then be permitted to participate in the Lord's Supper without his/her parent or guardian. This, like the developing Catholic, Anglican and Presbyterian practice places greater responsibility on the family and allows for greater individuality in response.[34]

In the United States the relationship of confirmation to first communion is a dilemma for the Lutheran who does not view confirmation as a completion of baptism but who wishes the communicant to commune in a worthy manner which has been historically related to the intellectual knowledge and commitment resulting from the whole process of confirmation. The issue is whether confirmation is really necessary for partaking of communion in a worthy manner. The unanimous decision of the Joint Commission on the Theology and Practice of Confirmation was that it is not. They further agreed that children in the fifth grade who are members of a Christian family are ready to commune and that confirmation would best be delayed until the tenth grade. The report states the following:

> Because of the tension between the educational demands of Holy Baptism and the Lord's Supper within the present practice of confirmation, the commission is unanimously moved to recommend that first communion and confirmation be separated as two distinct acts. This separation will allow children to partake of the Lord's Supper at an earlier age and then permit the church to carry on its pastoral and educational ministry through confirmation instruction at a time when Christian children are more mature.[35]

There is really nothing new in this idea for Lutherans. Melancthon and those who were with him had already been there at the meeting in Celle on November 16, 1548 when they agreed that in many instances first communion might well precede confirmation. The age recommended for confirmation was to be fourteen but Melancthon adds the following comment:

> The aforementioned age is not to be understood as though children of younger years who have been instructed in the catechism may not be brought by their parents to confession and the sacrament in accordance with the passage, Let the children come to Me, for such belong to the kingdom of God. But confirmation shall take place at an age of discretion when the children better understand their faith and their affirmation.[36]

And thus Lutherans join the ranks of those who endorse the baptism/communion/confirmation rubric.

The Reformed Tradition

In Scotland during the sixteenth century there was no ecclesiastical prescription regarding the age for admission to first communion. We do know that John Knox (1505-1572), while a minister of St. Giles in Edinburgh, admitted a boy of ten to communion[37] and in the "Miscellany of the Maitland Club" an event is recorded that occurred in the Edinburgh Presbytery of the Reformed Church in Scotland in 1575. Janet Aikenhead, a ten year-old girl, so the account goes, got into Edinburgh Castle with a married woman. She was detained and summoned before the Presbytery. Because of her age she was not punished and was admitted to the table of the Lord without any satisfaction penalty.[38] During the same year, however, the Kirk Session of St. Andrews set the minimum age for admittance to the Lord's Table at sixteen.[39]

During the sixteenth century even non-communicants were urged to attend Holy Communion in Scotland. For example, the Glasgow Presbytery Records of 1597 resolved that grammar school scholars should be present in the High Kirk "to hear God's world preached and the sacraments administered."[40] Non-communicant children's attendance at the Lord's Supper soon disappeared, however, not to reappear until the nineteenth century in the Scottish Church.[41] Typical of this later development was the order of the Aberdeen Burgh Council in 1664 "that no bairnes nor young children be brought to the Kirk till they be capable to hear the Word and attend the ordinances."[42]

During the seventeenth century special classes for catechumen were all but unknown. The same tests were required of first communicants as were required of older members: an adequate knowledge of the Christian faith and the doctrine of the sacraments satisfactory to the session of the kirk and the ability to examine oneself and to renew the covenant of baptism.

James VI was anxious for all young people to be admitted to communion by fourteen as reflected in the fourth Article of Perth. Some, during this period were, in fact, younger. James Melville communed at twelve, Robert Blair at eleven and John Livingston at less than fourteen.[43]

One can see from these brief statements that, first, there was no prescribed age in the Church of Scotland for first communion. Second, there was no specific ritual that opened the door to first communion. And, third, the only requirement for admission seemed to be an intellectual understanding of the Christian faith and a sincerity in the desire to communicate. Both the knowledge and the sincerity were to be evaluated by the session of the kirk in which the child was to commune.

The Reformed Church on the continent differed only in that confirmation based upon the same criteria, knowledge and piety, was introduced by Bucer (1491-1551) in an attempt to meet the criticism of Anabaptist reformers that persons baptized in their infancy were being admitted to communion without an adequate knowledge of the Gospel and without a personal saving faith.[44]

In the United States the trend in the Presbyterian Churches is toward the early communion of baptized children. A part of the problem is that American Presbyterians have instituted, as the Continental churches did, a formal confirmation that has been perceived as an admission to communion. Presbyterians have begun to feel the same uneasiness about this situation as this writer has experienced when confronted with the inclusiveness of the invitation to commune. For example, what does one do with the statement in the Westminster Confession of Faith which states that "the visible Church... consists of all those throughout the world that profess the true religion, together with their children."[45] Certainly the Lord's Supper is the church in one of its most visible moments!

The United Presbyterian Church in its 183rd General Assembly in 1971 amended its "Book of Order" to read as follows: "The session is charged with maintaining the spiritual government of the congregation, for which purpose it has power... to permit baptized children of the church, when their families deem it appropriate, to receive the Lord's Supper with the congregation before such children shall have made formal profession of faith."[46] With this action the United Presbyterian Church joined with the majority of Christians in those faith communities that practice infant baptism in endorsing and practicing the baptism/communion/confirmation rubric. We will next ask what this history of children at the Lord's Table says to the Christian Church (Disciples of Christ).

The Christian Church (Disciples of Christ)

We have seen a remarkable similarity in the development of children's communion in those churches that practice infant baptism. This is not unexpected because they do have a similar problem, *viz.*, How wide does baptism open the door to the church? or When is a member a member? or Is a religious experience only valid if it is cognitively apprehended? The emerging consensus is being expressed by these churches in three ways: First, first communion should be observed at a younger age than previously practiced. Second, confirmation requires greater maturity than participation in the Lord's Supper. Third, greater freedom (and more responsibility) should be given to parents and their children to determine when the child should join his/her parents at the Lord's Table.

The movement in these directions has accelerated rapidly in the past fifty years. But beyond the historical curiosity, what has been and will be the response of the Christian Church (Disciples of Christ) to the excitement that has resulted from the rediscovery of the children in our midst? Will we simply say that this new development is just an extension of infant baptism and reject it out-of-hand as unscriptural, illogical and perverse? There are those among us who would. Later we will look at what our current practice is among Disciples churches but first let us consider what our practice seems to have been in the past. One must say "seems to have been" because it is difficult to make any statement of *de jure* fact regarding Disciples polity and the *de facto* statements are always blurred at the edges.

We have historically assumed a profession of faith at a variety of ages from early childhood to old age. The author made his own confession of faith and was baptized when he was barely eight and even in our churches where we try to regulate the age, usually around twelve, there are enough exceptions to make it impossible to establish any age as the appropriate time to take this significant step in ones spiritual journey. It is not because we don't have the courage to do this (we've been stubborn enough about immersion); it is because it seems inappropriate to do so even when a child comes forward to make his/her confession at an age we feel to be too young. The confession of faith is followed almost immediately, seldom more than a week, by baptism and communion.

Now the interesting thing about our children's confession of faith and the events leading up to it is the fact that it is remarkably and strikingly similar to confirmation as practiced in many churches even to the gift of the Holy Spirit. Most Disciples ministers pronounce a blessing for the child after the confession of faith such as "May God bless you in the confession you have made" or "May Christ's Spirit be with you as you seek to live the Christian life." Shades of Thomas Aquinas! He couldn't have stated the idea of *robur ad pugnam* (armed for the battle) better! Disciples' confirmation (confession of faith) not only captures the essence of medieval confirmation but it also partakes of its ancient significance as unconsciously demonstrated by holding the hand of the person making the confession as well as the modern idea of confirmation as the consciously deliberate acceptance of the faith in which one has been reared or to which one has been brought.

In a sense, Disciples restored the unity of the ancient baptism/confirmation/communion rubric while transposing it to confirmation/baptism/communion and since confirmation and baptism were so intimately related it would appear that there is little difference because they belong together. When one compares this to the emerging pattern of baptism/communion/confirmation in the larger segment of Christendom which has already been discussed, it appears that we Disciples are in a position to do what they cannot do (at least without some ecclesiastical discomfort) and that is to change the rubric to what I believe can be scripturally affirmed, theologically justified and psychologically verified, *viz.*, communion/confirmation/ baptism. We shall see in the second part of this study that this is exactly what Disciples are in the process of doing as we discover that the practice of our recent past that we consider traditional is more ecclesiastical than theological and dictated more by custom than the Bible.

The genius of Alexander Campbell is nowhere better shown than in his rejection of baptism as an initiatory rite and his insistence that it has only one purpose and that is "for the remission of sins" as a pledge and assurance of salvation through an act of submission.. Given our Disciples understanding of baptism and communion, therefore, it is not inappropriate to reject our "traditional" ordering of these events as more ecclesiastical than theological and more historical than biblical. We believe that the ordering of these events in the rubric of communion/confirmation/baptism is a natural consequence that is biblically justified, theologically responsible and pastorally appropriate.

PART II

There's Room at the Table

Report of 2000/2001 Survey
of the Christian Church
(Disciples of Christ)
Concerning

*The Role of the Child in the
Observance of the Lord's Supper*

✢ ✢ ✢

Report of 2000/2001 Survey of the Christian Church (Disciples of Christ) Concerning

The Role of the Child in the Observance of the Lord's Supper

During the winter and spring of 2000/2001 a survey was taken among the 3,770 congregations related to the Christian Church (Disciples of Christ) as determined by their listing in the Year Book & Directory, Christian Church (Disciples of Christ) to determine the practices of the Christian Church (Disciples of Christ) concerning the role of children in the Lord's Supper. In the letter accompanying the survey the reason for the survey was stated as follows:

Although I have looked at the issue in a variety of ways (biblical, theological, historical, psychological and educational), I now realize that I have very little current data on the actual practices, policies and beliefs of our Christian Churches regarding children's participation in the Lord's Supper.

You can be of tremendous help in filling in the picture of what is actually going on in our churches by completing and returning the enclosed survey/questionnaire regarding your own congregation's policies and practices.

An amazing 1,737 churches (46% of our congregations) responded to the survey indicating that the communion of children is an important issue among Disciples. The survey form and survey statistics are included in the appendices. The statistical summary and narrative summary are included in this report.

✢ ✢ ✢

Statistical Summary

The majority of those responding to the survey took the opportunity to make comments to clarify their responses, to justify their practices and to make statements or share experiences. Some of these were quite lengthy, some requiring additional pages. A sampling of these comments organized in several categories will be included in this report. The respondents were overwhelmingly clergy (84%) with board chairpersons, elders, secretaries, etc. accounting for the remaining 16%.

The basic question in the survey was this:

1. Do children in your congregation take communion prior to baptism?

867 (51.1%) checked yes to this question with an additional 218 (12.9%) checking both yes and no indicating that some unbaptized children do and others do not receive com-

munion. This would, of course, be true of almost any church that communes unbaptized children. The combined total 1085 (64%) makes a total of those whose churches commune unbaptized children approximately two-thirds with 36% checking no. In explaining their answers almost all of those who criticized the perceived ambiguity of the question answered it clearly.

It is interesting to note that even those churches that indicated they do not commune unbaptized children often make exceptions for special worship occasions such as Christmas Eve, Maundy Thursday, etc. These churches differentiate between those who regularly commune and those who occasionally commune. Others offer substitute elements such as fish crackers and grapes to avoid using wine (grape juice) and bread and thus obey the letter if not the spirit of what they believe to be doctrinal law. Others reported that children may take communion in the contemporary service but not in the traditional service or in children's church but not in the adult service. And many who do not make it a practice to commune children said that they would not make an issue of it during the service and some added that they would not even say anything to the parents later. A sizeable number of churches reported that they neither encourage nor discourage children's communion

The second question was:

2. Does your congregation have a common understanding or informal agreement on children's participation in the Lord's Supper?

This question is one that seeks to determine whether there is a perceived and accepted tradition in the congregation. It is an acceptance of "the way things are" or at least believed to be. It is often the assumption that the Christian Church

(Disciples of Christ) does not commune unbaptized children. Sometimes it is the assumption that children and their parents are going to do what they're going to do and so we take a *laissez faire* attitude. Or it may simply be that a congregation has found the communion of unbaptized children to be the natural response to our Lord's invitation. In each case it is non-reflective and requires no discussion. 70% of our congregations reported that there is an understanding regarding unbaptized children's participation in the Lord's Supper. 30% reported no such understanding or agreement.

The second part of this question asked, **If yes, does it** (the common understanding or informal agreement) **suggest participation or non-participation?** Of the 70% reporting a common understanding 61% said that their congregations' common understanding would be opposed to communing unbaptized children. This suggests that *many of our congregations are welcoming unbaptized children to the Lord's Table in spite of a perceived tradition opposing such a practice.* This obviously has the potential of conflict within congregations some of which was reported with great feeling especially by clergy both pro and con who find themselves on the opposite side of what they believe their congregations favor. One especially poignant letter was from a clergy person whose board of elders would not permit her to even return the questionnaire. I presume that the elders considered it a divisive issue not open to discussion or no one's business but their own.

The next question sought to determine how deliberately congregations either permitted or denied communion to unbaptized children:

3. Does your congregation have a formal policy regarding children's participation in the Lord's Supper?

Only 100 (6%) of our reporting churches have such a formal policy. And of these 100 churches 56 (58%) have a formal policy of non-participation while 41 (42%) have a formal policy of participation. Several congregations reported that they are considering such a formal policy to permit and even encourage unbaptized children to commune.

How can we account for so few churches having an "official" policy regarding the communion of children? Is it because of perceived tradition? Is it because it seems obvious to a congregation or that the church does not want to be the gatekeeper for the Lord's Supper? Is it because it hasn't occurred to anyone to question the status quo? Is it because children are not present during communion making it a non-issue? Is it because we have enough conflict in our churches without adding this to our agenda? I believe that many of our churches have a *don't ask, don't tell policy*. Many years ago I was advised by my senior minister not to bring this issue to the attention of the board of elders. The solution was to just let it happen. Of course this put the burden on the parents who had to decide with little or no guidance along with the approval or disapproval of other congregants and deacons who made the decision by the way in which they passed the communion trays. This brings us to the question of who makes the decision whether to commune unbaptized children and at what age.

The 4th question was:

4. If unbaptized children commune, at what age do they begin and who makes the decision, parents, pastor, elders, others?

66% of the total number of churches responding to the survey reported that it is the parents who make the decision whether their children will receive communion prior to baptism. This included a significant number of churches that do not commune children by intention but whose parents allow it anyway. Of those who commune unbaptized children an overwhelming 98% included parents in the decision and 88% of the decisions were made by parents alone. Others included in the decision were clergy, elders, grandparents, the church board, the church and, of course, the children themselves. The role of the clergy and elders in this decision making process can be seen in the statistical summary.

The majority of our churches are in agreement that it is a parental prerogative to determine if and when their unbaptized children will share in the communion service. Christendom in general is coming to a similar conclusion regarding the communion of unconfirmed and/or unbaptized children with parents having the "power to permit" as our Presbyteran brothers and sisters so aptly put it.

The results of the survey clearly indicated that there is a broad spectrum of beliefs and practices regarding the communion of unbaptized children among churches and within congregations. One issue that complicates communing children is our mobility among both congregations and denominations. If we accept infant baptism for children coming from other denominations where they have communed how can we deny unbaptized children who have grown up in our own denomination where infant baptism is not an option from sharing communion along with their young peers.

2370 churches responded to the question of when unbaptized children begin to receive communion in their congregations. Of these, 339 gave a specific age or a range of ages and 31 gave narrative responses. These are tabulated in the statistical portion of this report. Of those reporting specific ages at which children begin to receive communion, 45% begin during the pre-school years and 47% begin during elementary and high school years. The most favored age to begin communion is 6 to 8 years old with 35% favoring those ages. Adding the school grades and suggestive age according to the behavior of the child to the age groupings changes the percentages slightly as follows: birth to five – 52% and six to fifteen – 47%. This suggests that the age of first communion is somewhere during early childhood among those churches that do commune unbaptized children.

✢ ✢ ✢

Narrative Summary

Introduction

One of the more significant but less tangible results of the survey was the depth of feeling expressed regarding the issue of children at the Lord's Table. This was evidenced, first of all, by the high percentage of returns—46%. A second indication of the issue's importance to the persons responding was the number of additional comments that were included, many of them quite lengthy even requiring additional pages. 1003 (58%) of the respondents made additional comments. A third indication was the emotional intensity of the responses including personal and pastoral experiences sometimes at odds with their congregations as well as biblical, theological and personal rationales for their stance on the subject.

The survey allowed hundreds of people an opportunity to be heard, a kind of *Let it Out* opportunity so popular in our daily newspapers and talk shows. The stance of many congregations was that of "don't ask, don't tell" that some articulated with those very words. The survey also prompted a number of churches to officially deal with the issue that had been too long ignored and was causing problems within the church. What was happening was really important to these people and many felt a discomfort with what was happening in their churches, both those who favored and those who opposed the communion of unbaptized children and those who were torn both ways. A common plea was, "We need help!"

Where the Bible Speaks

One would think that Disciples, of all people, would look closely at the Bible to determine the propriety of communing children, baptized or not, and base their decision on that. Of the 1003 persons who added additional comments only 31 offered a specifically biblical rationale for their belief and practice other than a vague assertion that what was being done was either biblical or unbiblical. Of course, churches were not asked to make a defense of their practice but considering how many desired to explain their position it was surprising how few cited specific scriptures to support their beliefs. Even more surprising, more people (24) based their support of communing children on biblical grounds than did those who opposed it for biblical reasons (13).

The primary scriptural support for those who wished to commune children, baptized or not, was the passage from Mark 10:13-16 and repeated in Matthew 19:13-15 and Luke 18:16 that includes these words of Jesus, "Let the little children come to me; do not stop them; for it is to such as these that the Kingdom of God belongs (Mark 14b). This passage was cited 19 times although many more simply repeated the phrase "Let the children come." Other passages cited include the statement by Jesus in the institution of the Lord's Supper, "Do this in remembrance of me" (John 11:24-25); a reminder that children are "first" in the Kingdom of Heaven; Luke 17:2 in which Jesus says, "It would be better for you if a millstone were hung around your neck and you were thrown into the sea than for you to cause one of these little ones to stumble. [*I am surprised that this text was not also used as an argument against the communing of children rather than to support it*]; and one respondent who cited six texts without comment in a church that communes children: Mark 10:13-16, Ephesians 6:1-6, Psalm 127:3, Matthew 19:14, Romans 10:9-10, and John 3:16.

Those churches that do not believe unbaptized children should participate in the Lord's Supper cite Paul's words found in I Corinthians 11:27-29 seven times, "Whoever, therefore, eats the bread or drinks the cup of the Lord in an unworthy manner will be answerable for the body and blood of the Lord. Examine yourselves, and only then eat of the bread and drink of the cup. For all who eat and drink without discerning the body, eat and drink judgment against themselves." This passage focuses on the requirements that the communicant shares in communion in a worthy manner after examining himself and discerning the body. [*It is interesting to note that this scripture was the reason why more children participated in the Lord's Supper than adults during the Middle Ages because adults were fearful that they would eat in an unworthy manner but this was no cause for alarm for their children because their innocence protected them.*]

Other biblical texts cited only once include the following: I Corinthians 11:29-34 in which the communicant is admonished to discern the body of Christ in the Lord's

Children at the Lord's Table

Supper and to eat at home if hungry. I Corinthians 7:27-32 having to do with unmarried women and widows rather than children and communion. Matthew 9:17 and Luke 5:37 having to do with putting new wine into old wineskins are cited by two persons. In John 3:5 Jesus says, "Very truly, I tell you, no one can enter the kingdom of God without being born of water and Spirit." This is expanded to mean that no one can commune without first having been baptized. Another person says, "My Bible calls participants [in the Lord's Supper] 'believers' and assumes that children cannot be believers. Yet another quotes Mark 16:15-16 which includes the Great Commission and ends with these words, "The one who believes and is baptized will be saved; but the one who does not believe will be condemned," as a reason for not communing the unbaptized.

Another biblical argument is this statement: "Luke 22:20 teaches us that the Lord's Supper is a covenant remembrance. It is my belief therefore that it is reserved for those in covenant with God. If children partake before baptism they do so without awareness." Another pastor had this to say: "As per the teaching of the bible: 1. The communion with Christ was among the saints. 2. The saints were those who had confessed Christ." [*This was seen as sufficient to establish a de facto exclusion of children from the Lord's Table.*] A curious response that insisted on baptism before communion in spite of the Bible was this: "Baptism first even though biblically all who confess and believe are welcome to partake." [*Perceived tradition trumps the Bible in a congregation that does not commune children!*] Another pastor offers this:

> In trying to form my personal policy on this issue I draw from my American Baptist childhood in which in *no way* were you going to even touch the trays as they passed. But...in trying to use the Bible as my guide, I hear the Lord say, "Do this in remembrance of me." But could it be for those kids who have nothing to

"remember" "Do this to get to know me—know my body was broken for you—know my blood was shed for you." Then you have something to remember.

There were some who opposed communing children based upon the Bible without mentioning specific passages. For example, "As per the teaching of the Bible: 1. The communion with the saints was among the saints. 2. The saints were those who had confessed Christ."

The survey was disturbing to some because it appeared to be challenging strongly held beliefs and practices as summarized in the following comment from a pastor whose congregation is in agreement that unbaptized children should not receive communion: "I find this survey to be scary. It appears to me that the Disciples of Christ are preparing to dilute the Bible further. It appears to be another step towards establishing "church traditions" over and above the Word of God. I believe that the pattern established by Jesus and as recorded in the Bible should be our guide. The majority of people are always wrong. God's Word, the Bible, is always correct."

A third group of responses includes those who believe that "there is no scriptural reference for excluding children," bringing us to the second part of our oft quoted slogan, "Where the Bible speaks we speak, where the Bible is silent we are silent." One pastor puts it succinctly: "Scripture does not speak to this issue, so parents should help educate a child as to the reason and importance of this sacred event. To do otherwise wouldn't be Disciple."

A minister shared this story:

> I have just started ministry (1 month) and do not agree with the stance this congregation takes on communion. I have talked to the Elders about this matter. They insisted they retain their tradition but, "would not refuse communion to a child if the parent allowed the child to take communion." I am not aware of any

scripture that prohibits a child baptized or unbaptized from taking communion. As Disciples we say, "Where the bible speaks...." (Illinois pastor)

The same minister continues

One of the most beautiful images I have in my mind is visiting a worship service where a young mother took her eight-month-old child to the communion rail with her, because the father was not with them in worship that day. The pastor asked the mother to stand the child on the rail. The child stood there with very large, serious eyes. As the pastor broke the communion wafer and leaned toward the child, the child automatically opened his mouth and stuck out his tongue. The pastor gently placed a piece on the child's tongue. The child never took those large, serious eyes off the pastor during the entire process. If even an 8 month old can sense the seriousness or sacredness of such an event, how can humans deny access to any human being, especially when it is the Lord's table—not ours? (Illinois pastor)

Another minister responds in a similar way, taking it a little farther:

Our informal policy allows participation. Historically we have said, "Where the Bible speaks we speak; where the Bible is silent we are silent." Frankly, I find nowhere in the Bible that unbaptized individuals (of any age) are fenced from the table of Holy Communion. The only possible restriction that I find is that the communicant must "perceive the body and blood of Christ." I take this to mean that the communicant must believe that Jesus is the Christ, the Son of the Living God, and to see in this celebration a personal identification with him as personal Lord and Savior. But what about the very young? Jesus says, "Continually be helping the little children to be coming to me....." I believe that including these children in the experience may help them in their coming into the family of grace." (Kansas pastor)

Part II · There's Room at the Table

In Summary: As Disciples look at the Bible, some find support for communing all children in a statement of Jesus (Mark 10:13-16 and Matthew 19:13-15) and others find support for denying the Lord's Supper to all children in a statement by the Apostle Paul (I Corinthians 19:13-15). Several make their decision by drawing inferences from other scripture passages. Still others point out that nowhere in the Bible are children specifically prohibited participation in the Lord's Supper or commanded to do so. In looking to the Bible for a specific answer to this issue conscientious persons discover three answers: yes, no and maybe so!

✝ ✝ ✝

Church Tradition and Doctrine

If the Bible does not directly answer the question of children's participation in communion we are left with church doctrine and tradition on one hand and the spirit of the New Testament seen in our Lord's ministry and the faithful witness of his followers on the other. Doctrine attempts to be the latter but finds it difficult to bend with the Spirit. That is why Campbellites rallied around the slogan, "No creed but Christ!" That is why one pastor in response to the question about a formal policy responded, " Formal policy is creedal in nature, and therefore infringes on the Disciples' non-creedal heritage and foundation." Another pastor said, "We chose not to formulate an *official policy*, feeling that a policy, any policy, would not be in keeping with our restoration heritage. Yet another pastor put it this way:

> We would never put communion in a policy form—how sacrilegious! Let's put one more leash on God's body, let's try to control the freedom of God one more

time...NOT! God is having a hard enough time finding a way into our hearts without trying to limit him. We also serve communion to Hindus, Buddhists, Muslims, Jews and anyone else who is open to be touched by God's Christ. (Washington State pastor)

Another pastor saw my survey as an attempt to create a new creed and many others left it to the parents to decide no matter what their personal preference might be. That's why our non-creedal stance can result in stories such as this from the respondents:

Prior to my ordination, the church I was attending partook of communion by coming forward and kneeling. The children also came forward and were blessed but not allowed to take communion. One Sunday the pastor's 3-year-old son looked up as dad was about to bless him and asked, "Why doesn't God love me?" His father, the pastor, reassured him that God did love him, but the child doubted. He said, "If God loved me he would let me eat with the rest of the people." Out of the mouths of babes.... That child informed my understanding of who was to be included in this wonderful family meal! (Michigan pastor)

Not everyone, however, sees the "no creed but Christ" tradition of the Disciples as helpful. Here are several:

This is a subject of wide ranging differences, opinions, and behavior. Much of this comes from a lack of education, some from an unwillingness to "create a fuss." Church boards don't want a fuss with their Gen-X members. Our Disciples tradition of "no creed but Christ" makes insistence difficult. The attitude and response is, "If you don't want them to have it, then take it away and don't tempt them. Children's worship helps greatly if it is truly educational. (Tennessee pastor)

> As a pastor, one of my aspirations is to see a more uniform standard for children partaking in Holy Communion. The Lord's Supper is a very vital part of our Worship Service. Each member of our congregation needs to understand the significance of the special service. Therefore, it is my opinion, that until children have accepted [*Christ*], then go through an orientation period or training, we should not allow them to participate in these services. Taking a National stand and having one uniform rule for all Disciples would make it more enforceable. (South Carolina pastor)

> In other congregations I have served there has been a policy requesting that the unbaptized not partake. This congregation has always allowed the unbaptized to partake. This is the case even after I have shared in sermon or communion meditation to the contrary. A Free Church tradition allows for no uniform practice. We need to establish as a Church (denomination) the teaching that only "Baptized Believers" should participate. (Kentucky pastor)

> I do not serve the Lord's Supper to anyone known not to have been baptized regardless of age. (Georgia pastor)

A Kentucky pastor makes an interesting doctrinal distinction:

> When parents ask me about participation, I encourage waiting. However, if children do occasionally participate, I have no problem since I view communion as ordinance rather than sacrament...We are an inclusive community especially at the Lord's table.

From the responses it is clear that a large portion of Disciples believe that the doctrinal position of the Christian Church (Disciples of Christ) is that communion follows baptism. For example, a lay respondent writes:

We, as a congregation, feel that the Rite of Baptism goes hand in hand with the Rite of Baptism (immersion). When a child has reached the age that they are willing to accept Christ as their Lord and Savior, regardless of what that age may be, they then make their confession and are baptized and receive communion. I personally feel that the Christian Church (DOC) has become too liberal concerning the long-standing doctrines of our church. If we don't take a stand for something then we as a church stand for nothing. (Virginia lay leader)

This makes it difficult for pastors and congregations to challenge what they see as the tradition of our denomination. The problem is compounded by the fact that many of our families come from other denominations whose children have been baptized as infants and whose baptism we accept. If baptism is the ticket to communion these children cannot be denied communion with or without the understanding we require of believer's baptism. But what about the children who were born into our denomination and were not baptized as infants, receiving only a blessing at birth? Are they to be excluded while those baptized in another faith tradition are invited to commune? Or what about children who move from one Disciples church to another that has a different practice? And if this doesn't create a sufficient dilemma, what about pastors who in moving find themselves at odds with their new congregations? It is both a marvel and a testimony to the resiliency of our congregations and their ability to adapt to a multiplicity of theological views or at least to tolerate them with a measure of grace that we can hold all of this together in one body of believers with as little conflict as there is. We will look at some of the thoughts and feelings of those who struggle with this issue each week as their congregations gather about the Lord's Table.

One pastor made the following observation: "Interesting to note that the Commission on Theology refused to address the issue of children and communion when it prepared a statement for the General assembly a few years ago." An Illinois pastor wrote a lengthy rationale for the inclusion of children including this statement challenging the tradition of baptism before communion:

> I am quite passionate about this topic. The only reason, in my opinion, to forbid the unbaptized an invitation to the table is a rigid adherence on tradition that would associate baptism with an entrance requirement. By the late 1st Century, that was being done. Some notable liturgical scholars today define Christian as "a baptized person." I do not think a person can make the defense that in the early 1st Century, in the meal practices of Jesus, and in the community meals associated with Pauline communities, that baptism was a requirement for participation in the community meal. It seems to me that anyone was welcome (e.g., at Corinth sinners were present at what seems to be a symposium (I Corinthians 12—14). So, I would argue, that even from the viewpoint of tradition, baptism as an argument for participation in communion is a late 1st Century to early 2nd Century development at about the time the "meal" became "eucharist."

An Illinois pastor whose church does commune unbaptized children says, "The greater theological questions have to do with our understanding of "baptism" and "original sin" and "theology of grace" and "sacraments" and concludes that his position is that it is a matter of informed conscience. [*He included six pages of copyrighted material that he had prepared on baptism, grace and sacraments.*]

A Texas pastor cites the lack of clarity in Disciple tradition:

> Our congregation, like most, attempts to adhere to Disciple tradition and policy. But, at the same time, since Disciple tradition on not clear on this subject and since our denomination is so individually oriented and

tolerant, our policy is to allow individuals to determine this issue for themselves.

The tension between those who adhere to a heritage that suggests communion following believers baptism and those who disagree with the confession/baptism/communion rubric and those who oppose taking any doctrinal position at all creates a friction within the Disciples and within congregations that creates heat that quietly smolders among the faithful, breaking out in flame from time to time and place to place. For the most part, congregations would prefer to smother the issue without resolving it.

✢ ✢ ✢

How Open Should the Table Be?

The dilemma of an open table versus a table that has requirements of age, understanding and faith commitment elicited some of the strongest comments. We will let them speak for themselves beginning with a continuation of the previous statement from an Illinois pastor:

> My proposal for child participation:
>
> (1) "Understanding" communion is not the point. Participation or belonging is the point. From an epistemological standpoint, learning through experiencing is, I think, more effective. We should ask: What is it we feel is so important for children to "know" before participating in communion? And how best can they "know" it?
>
> (2) Culturally, I am encountering more and more "mixed" families (i.e., some children in the family from a marriage are baptized, etc.—you know). My question is, in urban areas or in multicultural rural areas, are

churches experiencing mixed-religions marriages? Will churches allow, for example, children raised Muslim to attend church with their new Christian mommy and take communion when the dad's still a Muslim?

(3) In a divided world such as ours—one frequently divided *because* of religious fundamentalism—the church has no better metaphor for God's dream for creation (i.e., kingdom of God) than an open table.

(4) Requiring baptism for participation in communion is disconsonant with Jesus' inclusive table practice, which, my bias is, provides the historical grounding for "communion," if that is to be considered important.

A California pastor claims that the questions on the survey are too structured for their congregation and proceeds to describe their way of including children:

> These questions are all too structured to apply to us. We have no "agreements" formal or informal about who may or may not take part in communion. Our statement, on ever Sunday bulletin, is: "Christ is the Host of the Table, and we are all His guests. Most children are in Children's Church at that time, but those present are certainly free to take part unless their parents disapprove. On Christmas Even, we have Communion with all ages present and most of the children present eat and drink of the elements. We are an informal congregation (rather than "high church"). A recent bulletin is enclosed showing our practice.

An Oklahoma pastor views inclusion both theological and educationally:

> Admittedly, this might reflect my views more than the church's but it has never been an issue or questioned in the four years I have been here. My understanding of communion is primarily theological and educational. Theological because the Lord's table is just that—His table (not mine, yours, or ours). And He invites **all** to his table. Who am I to refuse others his inclusive and

> welcoming table of grace? It seems to me that throughout the gospels, Jesus screamed the loudest about such an unwelcoming attitude. My view is also educational in the sense that participating children will eventually start asking questions such as: "Why do we do this?" and "What does this mean?" and "Is it important?" What a wonderful way to share the gospel.
>
> Think about the possible negative consequences of the opposite viewpoint. What are we communicating to children if we refuse to invite children to the table until "such and such" time or until "such and such" events occur in their life? What are we communicating? We are guilty of preaching grace and practicing works. Besides, when we are finally ready to allow our children to approach the table, guess what—they may no longer be interested in participating. We've lost them (at least for the time being). Hope these comments have been helpful.

Some believe that we can have it both ways with a number of individuals expressing this in a variety ways:

> We encourage children to wait until after baptism as part of their ritual of inclusion. However, we also practice radical inclusion in all parts of the church's life, so if a family wants to come to the Lord's Table together, they are welcome. (Arizona pastor)
>
> We have introduced communion in the children's Sunday school and have them participate at that time while the adults participate during worship time. (Arizona pastor)
>
> Children participate at the contemporary service. Those same children do not during the traditional service. The same people say the same words at both services. Interesting. What unspoken messages do we send in either setting? (Arizona pastor)

Others express their individual convictions:

Part II · There's Room at the Table

Over the years I have come to the position that the early church gathered around the table in worship. That meal has been metamorphosed into Transubstantiation, Consubstantiation, and In memoriam. In that I believe there isn't a church member in my church that would let anyone who came to their door go away hungry, therefore; I believe we should not deny any child a seat at God's table and let them go hungry. (Washington pastor)

I have been in the Disciples of Christ ministry for 32 years. About 10 years ago I gave the invitation to communion, "All who believe may partake." Then one very new family with 9 girls, ages 2 to 12, came and took communion. Their faith said, "They all believe in Jesus!" I have never made a distinction based on age since then! It is not an age issue; it is a belief issue. (Georgia pastor)

We do not exclude children from our family table at home; neither do we exclude them from the table of the family of Christ....It is more important for children to be full participants in the community which does this special thing for them than to be left out.
(Arizona pastor)

We believe the Lord's Table is open to one and all! (Arkansas pastor)

My personal belief, and the one I attempt to share with my churches, is that I'd rather have a child take communion with a slight lack of full understanding than to have them excluded. (Washington State pastor)

Thank you for this survey. Just last week a mother asked about her five-year-old son taking communion. I am a strong believer that the Lord's Supper is one that only those who have been baptized into Christ—adults or children [*should share*]. It needs to be understood how it came into being and it is serious business when we remember our Lord and Savior in the Bread and the Cup. It is not play time or let a child have communion to just keep them quiet. I think many parents do not understand the theology of the Table and how this is a time to remember our own baptism as we partake. Look to read your results.

I began my first pastorate 3 months ago, and I have a four-year-old son who keeps asking, "Daddy, why don't I get any juice?"…My personal feeling is that we need to find some way to include children. Theologically, if we considered the Lord's Supper a community meal, it would be appropriate to include children. If we interpret the Lord's Supper as an atoning sacrifice, however, we might draw another conclusion—that it is only for those baptized or old enough to know what they are doing. I am in the midst of a class on the Eucharist, and it seems to me like there is strong support for viewing the Lord's Supper more as a meal of the people, a meal where the family of God comes together to unite in fellowship and celebration and thanksgiving. (Tennessee pastor)

Parents will ask for my input. I encourage everyone to take communion! Can we really say that "Mary age 5" doesn't believe in Jesus with all her heart? Children love communion and at times are closer to the ritual holiness of it than adults. (Virginia pastor)

I am very open to children partaking at any age. Children do understand what it means to be welcome and included. Some of us experience God's grace at the table long before we commit to follow (baptism/discipleship). I have spoken to my elders and to parents who ask. Elders would not forbid. The decision of parents is respected. I simply cannot say "all are welcome" and then say, "except kids." (Iowa pastor)

Part II · There's Room at the Table

> My personal feeling is that if they truly understand communion then they would understand being baptized. So I don't like to have them partake, but without a policy it happens. Most of my members feel the same as I do, I think. Younger members allow their children to partake because it is easier to let them than it is to explain to them why they shouldn't. (Iowa pastor)

> I cannot in my wildest imagining picture Jesus excluding children. The understanding of what is occurring continues to mature over time but all are invited to participate at their level of understanding. We do not exclude the mentally handicapped. (Iowa pastor)

> The love demonstrated by Jesus for children would, I believe, be violated if children were excluded. They might not know the full import of the sacrament, but they will be taught, and in the meantime they are one with the congregation. (Kansas pastor)

> If God's grace welcomes and loves all, then the table which is the reflection of such good news, welcomes all as well. (Kansas pastor)

> I don't want to leave someone out of the feeling of grace....I have known several young children who have a far better communication with God than many adults. They know God; not just know about God. (Arkansas pastor)

A Tennessee church has solved the problem of inclusion in this way:

> We dedicate all our children and thus they are part of the covenant—so each family can decide when their kids are ready.

The ambivalence of many pastors is captured in this statement from a Virginia pastor:

> My observation is that some deacons offer communion to the children and sometimes the parents (or the adult

sitting with the child) will say, "No." Otherwise, the child takes communion. We have not discussed this as a church and perhaps we should. I have mixed feelings on the issue myself. My child has not yet been baptized and I'd prefer that he wait but in my communion invitation I simply say, "All believers in Christ are invited to participate." That would include my 7-year-old son! How can I deny him that?

The pastor of an Hispanic congregation in Texas reports that his congregation is totally inclusive in a letter accompanying the survey.

> [*Name of church*] is a diverse community serving people with a variety of religious backgrounds. There are more than 13 denominations represented in the community, there are Catholics, there are Episcopalians, there are Mormons, there are even agnostics.
> We do not subscribe to the notion that communion is only for Christians, and only for Christians that believe certain things about the sacrament.
> Foundationally, for our community it is a celebration of our journey together in God. We celebrate Christ as one who has revealed God's love, awakened us to a new experience of living, brought us together and holds us together as a community of faith.
> Communion reminds us of our oneness with God, one another, and all creation.
> No confession that Jesus Christ is Lord is required.
> Consequently, children are encouraged to participate because it's a celebration—a weekly celebration of God's love for us, our community, and our unity with all humanity and all creation.
> We have children under 2 years of age that participate. We have young children that serve...they understand that the table represents God's invitation to humanity to receive God's love and share it with others.

Other voices for inclusion follow:

Part II · There's Room at the Table

We feel the table is open to all. We do not attempt to regulate who can take. The decision is left up to those receiving, not those serving. Christ's message and ministry was and is open to all, so our table is open to all. (California pastor)

If children are included in heaven before baptism (which is our reason for not baptizing infants) who can exclude from the table those whom heaven includes? (California pastor)

Usually a parent will come to me to ask about their child having communion. We'll discuss it, but I usually leave it up to the parents. Usually on Christmas Eve and Maundy Thursday a larger number of children share in communion. Part of my reason for openness toward unbaptized children (and adults for that matter) being free to share in communion has to do with who was at the Last Supper participating in that meal. Judas Iscariot was still there and if the very institution of the Lord's Supper was open to him, who am I to tell anyone they cannot share in the Meal of Remembrance? Another part of my reason for allowing unbaptized children to have communion is that I don't want being allowed to have communion to be the "carrot" we hold out to them so they'll be baptized. (Oregon pastor)

I am strongly in favor of a theology of the table as open to all, a family gathering where no one is excluded. Participation should not be based on cognitive understanding or even a certain benchmark of faith. It is a place to meet Christ. (Colorado pastor)

The Table is not to be exclusive. Any statements regarding communion need to be inclusive. The invitation is from Jesus, not the church. As persons grow in discipleship they become more discerning regarding participation.

Children at the Lord's Table

Participation by children in communion suggests in this congregation:
1. They are part of the community.
2. Community as family, all included in all aspects of church life.
3. Parents will explain what the service means.
4. Parents will not pressure children to participate.
(Texas pastor and worship committee member)

As a pastor I do not exclude anyone from communion. Children have a unique way of seeing and understanding faith issues, as we know. Communion is a place and time for children to participate in our common belief that the Lord's Supper is for all persons who believe in Jesus Christ as their Saviour. Children do not have grownup answers about Jesus, salvation, etc., but they do believe at their level of understanding that the supper is very special and they want to participate. (Missouri pastor)

The Table is a gift to all! Jesus is a gift to all! (Missouri pastor)

When we sit at our dinner table do we deny our children food even if they are sitting at a card table?
It isn't that we encourage children to take communion before baptism, we just want them to feel like they are a part of the family of God.
It is through the breaking of bread that we come to know Christ. (Nebraska pastor)

I am uneasy about this participation. (The previous pastor included children.) But it is something I feel I cannot take away from them. They are active participants and they feel a part of worship. I would not have implemented it, but I feel I can't change the decision either. (Ohio pastor)

Part II · There's Room at the Table

This is something I care about as I worry what message of exclusion the children will receive. I have talked with the elders and there is not much agreement or disagreement (they just look at me). (Ohio pastor)

Each Sunday we print in the bulletin: "All God's children—young and old—may share in the Holy Meal. You may partake of the Loaf and the Cup as they are passed to you by the Deacons." (A decision made by the elders!) (Ohio pastor)

We did a formal study on this subject with the Elders and developed a theological affirmation of an open table. The Elders were unable to get the affirmation ratified by the Board, but we are practicing allowing unbaptized children/adults to share the supper of Jesus. I think prolonged Biblical and historical study needs to be presented on a congregational level. (Ohio pastor)

We apply the example of Jesus in Mark 10:13-16 as overriding any denominational rule or practice. (Oklahoma pastor)

Children under five are in nursery care so the beginning age is five-years-old. The Lord's Table is for everyone. This should never be a battleground. This prevents children from getting baptized so they can receive the communion. They will feel welcomed and a part of the faith community. Grace. (Oklahoma pastor)

The Lord's Supper belongs to the Lord, not to the church or to rules that exclude. It's about grace, not law. Jesus said to let the children come to Him and not to hinder them. How dare we keep the children from the most intimate and important sharing in our Lord that we participate in as a whole church? Communion is about grace, not law. We remember Jesus, not Moses. (Oklahoma pastor)

Random thoughts of the Pastor: 1) Children need to be included in the church family, not excluded. 2) Our practice of deferring participation until baptism may induce premature decision to be baptized in order to feel "grown-up." 3) It just feels right. (Oklahoma pastor)

When I first encountered the idea of allowing non-baptized children to partake of communion I had an extreme negative reaction. But over the past 12 years I have been persuaded that all people baptized or not are welcome at the Lord's table. If we believe this table is about forgiveness of sins and reconciling of people to God and each other then to withhold communion from someone is to withhold forgiveness. (Oklahoma pastor)

The table is a conduit of God's grace and I do not feel empowered to deny its experience to anyone. (Texas pastor)

Although they [*children*] don't understand the significance [*of communion*] they do understand being left out. Our approach is not to make an issue of it. When they approach baptism they will know the meaning. (Virginia pastor)

When you brought your child home from the hospital as a baby, did you wait until he was able to understand the principles of nutrition before you fed him? Or did you feed him and explain as he grew? Children need to feel a part of the worshiping community. (Texas pastor)

The table is an important symbol of the inclusion of all God's children. My family once attended a Lutheran church and went forward for communion. My 6-year-old daughter very carefully watched what others did and followed suit, kneeling with outstretched, expectant hands. When she received a pat on the head and a blessing instead of a wafer, she was very confused and disappointed. We encourage parents to include children as we feel this was the practice of Jesus in his ministry regardless whether children were present at the Last Supper. (Oregon pastor)

Our stance is Christ came to feed the hungry. All who are hungry are welcome to eat. We invite everyone to the table and openly make no distinction between the baptized and the unbaptized. (Oregon pastor)

Raised and baptized a Disciple, I was brought up in the withholding tradition. Allowing my children to take communion was a difficult decision that came only after much prayer. I do fervently believe it is the right thing to do, but I am greatly troubled by the lack of clarity and agreement throughout the church on this issue. It pains me to see that which is so central to our identity become so muddled in tension and division. (New Mexico pastor)

I think there is a lot of commonality within the Disciples of Christ in regard to participation in the Lord's Supper after baptism. But since historically we hold to a strong stance, "We neither invite nor debar," then our footing is on a slippery slope to be dogmatic. It is the Lord's Table, and it is Jesus who invites, not humans. I find as a pastor participation in the Lord's Supper by children serves as a wonderful teaching opportunity therefore teaching the significance of this wonderful sacrament and proclaiming the Lord's death until his return (as said by the Apostle Paul).
I have recently had a change of thought about this. When I invited "all who believe" to partake, I saw many believing little faces. An elders meeting is scheduled…to begin a process of discernment on this issue. [from the pastor of a congregation that does not commune children]

A Kentucky pastor and parent shares her struggle with this issue:

> We have taken communion with children in children's group as a teaching tool and to help the children in their curiosity about communion. I, too, struggle with this issue. The scripture that haunts me about this is Christ's calling the children to Himself and telling the disciples "to hinder them not." The other side of the coin is that communion is a holy sacrament that requires some understanding on the part of the participants. As a Christian educator, I always believed children should participate in worship more fully. Now, as a parent of a 5-year-old and a 7-year-old, I realize that there are times when we make things more powerful and meaningful by waiting. It is a dilemma. Experientially, as we stood in a circle taking communion in a small gathering, as I looked into the expectant eyes of my child, I could not deny her communion regardless of the depth of her understanding. The Spirit communicates with us in ways we cannot always see or understand. And, after all, how much do we (lifelong scholars) really understand the depths of the Spirit in communion?

The question, "How open should the Table be to children?" begins a passionate debate among Disciples for whom the Table is many things—remembrance, thanksgiving, sacrifice, obedience, forgiveness, fellowship, *anamnesis* (re-experiencing the Lord's Supper), presence, reward, sacrament; nourishment and whatever need I have that God through Christ can fulfill Some would require an act of obedience (baptism), some would require confession (examine yourself), some would require a certain level and kind of understanding, almost all would require parental approval. Some would simply say, "Whoever will may come." The fact that we have not succeeded in codifying the Lord's Supper is a reminder that it is, indeed, a mysterious gift of God through Jesus Christ whose Spirit governs the Table.

✢ ✢ ✢

How Much Do We Need to Know to Participate?

How much understanding (cognitive knowledge) is required to participate in the Lord's Supper? Or is there another kind of knowledge (affective, emotional, psychological social or spiritual) that is gained through participation in the Lord's Supper? Understanding is often used as a criterion for participating in the Lord's Supper but without defining understanding. For example, pastors often say, "My main encouragement to parents is the importance of participation with understanding. From the wide range of ages at which children receive their first communion it is obvious that there is little unanimity on this issue that is left primarily to parents to decide. A California pastor begins the discussion:

> I have pastored this congregation for less than a year at this time and I have had to initiate several discussions

to gather the information you requested (rather than simply provide you with my viewpoint). What I found in the conversations I had with others is that we have no written "policy" concerning communion. We definitely have individuals with strong opinions as to what they feel is proper. Yet, those opinions seemed primarily based upon experienced traditions—not upon any scriptural or theological conclusions that they had sought out or drawn for themselves. We also have other individuals who are mot concerned that there be an understanding by the participants of just what is taking place...*understand* this great mystery?

Our bulletin invitation to communion states, "If you are a believer that Jesus is the Christ, the Son of the Living God, then it is Christ himself who invites you to this Table of Remembrance and Thanksgiving." That invitation seems to indicate that we are not going to fence the Table according to our personal, or corporate judgment concerning another's relationship with Christ, but we expect and teach that they are to ascertain the significance of the invitation to receive Christ into themselves.

The reality of our unwritten "policy" is that we leave the decision concerning child participation in the Eucharist entirely up to the parents of that child. Even those congregants with strong objections to the non-baptized participating in this act of worship admit that they would not challenge the family's decision—though it did seem obvious that they would like for me to do so.

My experience with my own children was to discourage participation in the ordinance until such time as they could provide an explanation of the event being celebrated. I believe that their acceptance of Christ as Lord came in great part through their consideration of the gift of Jesus presented at the Table...and their public baptism came later, in response to their embracing the gift.

Part II · There's Room at the Table

> Recently, Xavier, a five year old—who, along with his parents, had been participating with our church body for only five or six seeks—left to go to Children's Church for the first time in all those weeks. While busying himself with all the program trappings we implement to teach our children the meaning of the gospel of Christ, he suddenly looked up at his teacher and asked, "Isn't it time to go back to church? I don't want to miss the body and blood of Jesus."
>
> Though punch and cookies were available in Children's Church, Xavier seemed to know there was something much more significant in the bread and cup found in the sanctuary. I hope we can *nourish* his insight...*with Jesus*.
>
> Who was it that said, "Let the little ones come unto me."?

Other pastors and lay leaders share their views:

> When my child was six-years-old, he and I were sitting together for communion. He tapped me on the shoulder and asked, "Can I have communion?" Since he had not been baptized (that's another question—at what age might that happen?), I asked him what he thought it meant to take communion. He responded, and I quote, "It means you know God loves you and you are going to try to love others." Should he have been allowed to receive communion? I made the decision to not stand in the way of the grace that he, somehow, at age 6, already knew about. He is now 13, was baptized at 11, and enjoys receiving communion to this day. (Oklahoma pastor)

> I encourage families to include all children who want to come. Mothers with small children will often carry them and a child may have a piece of bread or both bread and juice. The one thing they understand is exactly what we say—*all* are included—*all* are welcome. Sometimes a parent chooses not to have their child

participate. I leave it up to them. But, if a parent tells me, "They don't understand it," I respond, "They do understand what it means to be excluded. If they are a part of our family, they are always welcomed at the table." I also acknowledge that our understanding of communion changes over time, and perhaps many who come initially come with little understanding except that they are welcomed. After all, we encounter a mystery. Can anyone say they completely *understand* it? It is not so much an issue of understanding but, rather, experiencing a relationship with the One who loves us. Sometimes we experience that through other people as they welcome us. Even a child understands that. (Indiana pastor)

This, too, has been an issue of practical theology with which I've wrestled for years. I have reached a point of realizing that faith is both head *and* heart. Do I believe God is in children's lives? Absolutely. Do I believe children are capable of experiencing God and sharing in God's grace? Absolutely. Do I believe faith demands certain beliefs for communion to be effective? No. Does the inclusion of children at the central moment of worship in the celebration of God's grace help children experience and know God's full love? I believe it does. (Kansas pastor)

We do ask parents to be sure that the child knows that communion helps us to remember that 'Jesus loves us.' Older children are expected to know that 'Jesus died for us.' (Indiana pastor)

Innocence carries its own wisdom, perhaps more pure than what we've garnered with maturity. It is our notion that children learn by doing. (Washington State pastor)

Children are a part of the household of God and, although they need to be taught a gradual appreciation for the meaning of ritual, they need and deserve to decide to participate in communion even if at first they just don't want to be left out. (Washington State pastor)

It seems to us that the Bible does not support the idea that one must be baptized before one may take communion. Obviously, both baptism and communion should be "understood" by participants. However, we think that even a very young child can understand what communion means—at least on the level of "belonging to the community and to the Lord." (Texas pastor)

I believe children show an incredible understanding of what communion means. If we instituted a test, the kids might pass and adults fail. Now that could cause a problem! (Kansas pastor)

If they participate real early in age, they will never understand the true meaning of washing our sins away and starting a new beginning. (Kentucky lay leader)

The only reason I've ever heard for denying communion to children was that they didn't understand the meaning of the meal. But by that logic we would have to deny communion to a Catholic or a Lutheran who might have an understanding different from our own. I certainly understand this meal differently than I did when I had my first communion at age 12. If children understand nothing else, they understand that this is a meal shared by the family we call the children of God. Since they, too, are children of God, they should be welcome at Christ's table. (Ohio pastor)

We follow the Greek Orthodox idea that learning is in all five senses. We restrict nobody. (Maryland pastor)

We all understand the mystery of the Lord's Supper in our own way. Spiritual development is not necessarily

> a product of chronological age or religious training. (Massachusetts pastor)
>
> A form of evangelism is the allowance of children, no matter the age, to participate in the rituals and practices of the congregation including the taking of communion. (Michigan pastor)
>
> Children before age 12, I don't believe, have any concrete knowledge of why they would take communion. We don't want them to do it because they see others doing the same. At age 12, as Jesus was about His Father's business, so shall the children be taught in greater depth of a commitment to Jesus Christ. [*Baptism is the requirement for communion in this congregation.*] (Missouri pastor)
>
> Someone said, "Children need to understand what it means"—another said, "So, do we tell children not to say the Lord's Prayer until they know what it means?" The elders decided to leave the issue to the parents and the child. (Ohio pastor)
>
> It scares me when children aren't taught to wait! If children are permitted to be a part of that rite before their maturation there is a lack of understanding or purpose. (Ohio pastor)
>
> Children are allowed to participate in communion when they have a moral understanding of what is right and wrong.

An Illinois pastor writes more fully with an appreciation of conflicting views:

> Based on our practice of infant dedication and inclusion of children from church families and our open stance at The Lord's Table it always seems to me that children who are 7 or 8 could partake **if** we stressed the idea of

> inclusion and of God's grace operating in their lives before they have full understanding. Most children can understand "This is the family meal" and "I am part of the family because I was born into a church and family." They can say, "I love Jesus."
> Our general practice is to tie communion to their confession of faith and baptism that emphasizes their *understanding of symbolism* and their readiness to own their own faith and make their own decision.
> I see value in both. I think because Disciples have never been concerned about a child's "salvation status" before baptism and our emphasis on "understanding," that most of the five churches I have served have leaned more to the latter practice.
> One could also point out that since all of us are on a spiritual journey and our understandings continually change and deepen that no one can say they "fully understand" the mystery.

An elder of another congregation equates the understanding needed for baptism and for participation in communion:

> It has been the informal consensus of our church leadership for many years that the growth and development of spiritual maturity needed for children/youth to decide for Christ in baptism is equally essential in the comprehension of the partaking/sharing/remembrance of the Lord's Table. We are convinced that an informed and understanding commitment of baptism into the Fellowship of Christ must precede the invitation to Communion.

A Missouri pastor provides a glimpse of the thinking and theological reflection behind her church's practice:

> Our congregation is not all of one mind on this issue. However the vast majority and most of those with children believe that children should be welcome to participate fully at the Lord's Table. The issue has been

discussed within the eldership and diaconate and the decision made that children (unbaptized) are welcome and that their participation is up to parental discretion. We have a few older members who believe that only baptized (or confirmed, if baptized as an infant) children should receive communion. Respecting that stance, we have still arrived at the conclusion that the Table of Christ is open to all. The Table is the place where all are received wherever we may be in our faith journey. The Lord's Supper is not something we earn by virtue of a particular level of understanding. We as Disciples of Christ believe that children are embraced in God's grace *before* they are baptized. We have never feared for the salvation of a child if that child were to die before confession of faith and baptism. Therefore to say that a child is not welcome at Christ's Table because of being unbaptized makes no sense.

A member of our congregation raised an excellent point when she was responding to the argument that a child does not "understand" communion. She said, "Who does? It is a mystery. And children may have a greater openness to the mystery and presence of God than adults do." Another brought up the fact that the congregation includes persons who are emotionally and mentally disabled and who are assumed to be welcome at the Table because they have been baptized. We cannot know what they "understand" of either their baptism or communion! What we do know is that they *experience* being a part of Christ's community of Love. So it is with children! Who can judge that one kind of understanding is better than another; that one kind of understanding qualifies us for the Table and another does not.

A Tennessee pastor captures the dilemma of some churches basing their preferred practice not on understanding but upon relationship:

> We do not encourage non-baptized children to commune, but we have not found an easy way (that would be diplomatic and positive) of telling parents to restrict them. Sharing the Lord' Supper is a wonderful experience, but I believe it is much more meaningful and an actual experience with God through Jesus when it is within the context of a relationship. The New Testament seems to indicate that this relationship is one between a baptized believer and Jesus Christ. We love our children enough to encourage them to enter this kind of relationship; then to experience the fullness of the joys, opportunities and responsibilities thereof.

The question, "How much do children need to understand to participate in the Lord's Supper," raises a host of questions: How much does one need to understand to be a Christian? How much does one need to understand to be baptized? Our understanding is always in need especially when the object remains a mystery that can never be fully known, leaving us always needing to know more. So the question becomes, What is the minimum level of understanding that opens the gate to the Lord's Supper and what is it and who determines it? Disciples have either by default or wisdom left this decision to the child's parents for the most part while acknowledging that communion after baptism has been the norm. Or is understanding discovered in the act itself? If this is so, then it is a most serious matter to deny anyone access to the Table. And so the argument goes on in our churches but even within the uncertainty, conflict and agitation old truth is rediscovered and new understanding evolves rising to the surface of our life together to enrich and nurture the whole church.

Accommodating Our Diversity

Nowhere is Disciples ingenuity more evident than in the ways in which they have accommodated diversity alongside strongly held opinions regarding children's participation in the Lord's Supper. Even in those churches that do not commune unbaptized children, ways have been found to allow participation in creative, imaginative and practical ways that do not violate real or imagined policies to the contrary and to make acceptable compromises and exceptions without undue notice or disturbance.

The first compromise is to do nothing to prevent a child from communing even when it is not the practice of the church. A few random comments from the survey will illustrate this common expedient:

> We do not snatch the elements away from children, but our church congregation believes that communion is for those who have confessed Christ and been baptized.

We do not promote children taking communion before baptism but would not slap their hand if they didn't know any better.

They [*the congregation*] insisted they retain their tradition but "would not refuse communion to a child if the parent allowed the child to take communion."

Parents are allowed to commune their children but they know how we feel.

Should a child partake we do not get huffy about it nor does Jesus.

Non-participation is our policy, but no fuss is made if children want to.

We do not embarrass visitors or non-members by refusing to serve children.

We don't formally deny a child communion.

The elders have passed a policy asking that children not commune until they are baptized or confirmed, but this has been generally ignored.

We've seen a few children (unbaptized) take communion when parents (sometimes unbaptized) permitted—always when they were new to Disciples and/or church! Should never risk embarrassing or hurting feelings by refusing what is Jesus' to one of his children.

One can only speculate the reason why congregations do not enforce what they perceive to be the tradition of the Disciples and the accepted practice of their congregations. Is it out of fear of offending a vital segment of our community—young families? Is it because the issue just isn't that important? Is it because we wish to avoid conflict? Is it a hospitality issue? Is it uneasiness with the tradition? Whatever the reason Disciples are loath to prevent the practice of unbaptized children communing at the Table.

Children at the Lord's Table

The second compromise is fairly common and that is to commune children at specific times or special worship services and to deny them communion at other times. Here are some examples from the written comments:

> Children participate at the contemporary service. Those same children do not during the traditional service. Interesting....What unspoken messages do we send in either setting?
> We have two services. It is like two separate churches. The answers [*to the questions on the survey*] for each service are different. (Ohio pastor)

> Several times a year we hold a circle communion (agape) where everyone is invited to partake. On regular Sundays we use matzo and grape juice, in pieces and individual cups. For circle communion we use Hawaiian king's bread (a soft round loaf that holds together well). The bread is passed and each takes a piece and dips it in the cup. Children of all ages are invited to participate in this "feast:" as Jesus taught us on the mountain. The Communion/Last Supper is reserved for believers who wish to be nurtured by Christ's fruit and nourished by this opportunity. Wine and grape juice in marked chalices are offered at the Good Friday Service where the Table is "open" and people, sometimes individually and as families come forward, kneel and partake, leaving when they are "emptied" and "filled."

> At Maundy Thursday and Christmas Eve (both communion services) I, the minister, ask that if the family would like for their children to share in taking communion, it is acceptable. During the rest of the year, children do not share in the communion (except to watch).

> Usually two times a year, Maundy Thursday and Christmas Eve, when we actually come to the table and dip bread into the chalice kids are welcomed. I believe this is good. Jesus said, "take and eat" and "drink of it all of

you." It also alleviated desire for baptism just to partake of communion.

For Thanksgiving we will have wafer like cookies in the bread tray as a way for unbaptized children to participate in the sacrament.

For World Communion Sunday this year, about a third of the way through the service, we processed—singing—to Fellowship Hall where we had communion with the "whole family of God." Howard Ratcliff (Regional Minister of Ohio) led our Communion and we were served slices of various breads and glasses of white grape juice on serving trays. I don't like to exclude children, but I also see the value of having them wait for understanding. This day was an exception and appreciated by most.

During the summer months we have all the children take communion in their second hour children's worship service. They are taught the basis of worship at that time. Throughout the rest of the year communion is brought in to second hour and the children are reminded it is for those who have been baptized. (Oregon pastor)

Somehow if one doesn't commune children often and if it's only on special occasions or in different settings it is not seen as a violation of the general practice of the congregation. These exceptions take place on a variety of occasions with Christmas Eve and Maundy Thursday being the most frequent. Other days include Easter, World Communion Sunday, Thanksgiving, Christmas and Good Friday. Other settings rather than the "regular" worship service include the Saturday evening praise service, contemporary services, all church retreats, family camp, children's church and Sunday school. The surprising thing about these exceptions is that they are well received because they are not considered as precedent setting in churches that wish to retain the traditional practice.

A third compromise is to substitute the traditional grape juice (fermented or unfermented) and bread (leavened or unleavened) with something else. For example:

> We have "goldfish" in the plate with the communion bread. On the plus side, it includes the children in the sacrament and they seem to be serious about it.

> Sometimes the deacons will include a few cups of water in the tray for children who think they're not quite ready for the "real thing."

> Kids get grapes as soon as they can understand the words, "God loves you."

> We serve raisins to children.

> They [*children*] participate with grapes once a month.

> We have added an aspect t our Communion Service which allows persons who are not Christian (children and adults) to share in the meal with us. In addition to the Bread and the Cup we now also have grapes. The grapes, also from the vine, express our hope that one day they too will accept Christ as Lord but recognizes that because they are also created by God they are precious to Him now—and that He desires that they be saved. This is not original with us. In visiting [*an Hispanic congregation*], I was introduced to this and adapted it for our congregation. I can say in just over two months it has helped us maintain the sacredness of the meal and at the same time include others. (Pennsylvania pastor)

> Children are allowed to eat the bread and drink the juice after the service. [*In another context the Canaanite woman said, "Yes Lord, yet even the dogs eat the crumbs that fall from their master's table (Matthew 15:27).*]

> We have a family worship service once a month on Wednesday evening. At this service we celebrate a

> "meal" together of grapes and animal crackers. Everyone takes part in this.
>
> When we expect large numbers of small children to be present (Christmas Eve and special services), I have special food given to them with a blessing.
>
> On the fourth Sunday of each month the elementary children act as liturgists. They also distribute fresh grapes at the same time as the deacons distribute communion. The practice was started in Junior Worship because some parents did not want their children to partake of the elements but some of the children were feeling left out. The grapes are a way everyone regardless of age or membership can be part of the community gathered that day.
>
> Each child receives a blessing as communion is passed.
>
> We let small children have a small box of raisins signifying the fruit of the vine.

Grapes and goldfish crackers along with raisins and animal crackers are a popular substitute for the bread and wine of communion. For some reason, using non-traditional foods for children at the Lord's Table makes the children's participation sufficiently different from the baptized person's participation in the more traditional manner acceptable. One cannot help but note that grain is grain and the fruit of the vine is the fruit of the vine no matter in what form they are served. But it does have the beauty of making the inclusion of children doctrinally permissible to the congregation if not logically consistent.

Whatever one might think of these three compromises they do allow congregations to accommodate diversity in the inclusion of children at the Lord's Table with a minimum of disturbance to the congregation.

✢ ✢ ✢

Education for Communion

How best to prepare children to participate in communion at the appropriate time and to continue that learning into adult life is as varied as most Disciple practices. We must remember that the survey did not ask how children are prepared for communion so the lack of comments does not imply a lack of such preparation. However, among the volunteered comments we find at least six educational practices that can be listed under these general headings:

1. Observation
2. Participation
3. Parental guidance and conversation
4. Pastoral counseling, and instruction
5. Organized classes
6. Written policies or directives

1. **Observation** relies on the premise that children will learn adult behavior from observing what adults do. There

is also the hope that children will gain adult understanding by listening to, as well as watching, adults participate in the Lord's Supper. This may be true but a California pastor reminds us, "Rarely are our children still in worship when Communion is observed." This is probably true of the majority of our congregations. A Georgia pastor makes a case for observation: "I do believe children participate in the Lord's Supper as part of the community expectant—they are being taught and prepared for their own communion" by witnessing the faithful, obedient Body of Christ "do this in remembrance" of the Lord.

2. **Participation** may take a variety of forms. As we have seen participation on a few occasions and in special settings but not regularly is quite common and is seen as educational. As an Alaskan clergyperson says, "The act [*communion*] itself is educational," and two California clergypersons say, "We like to think of it [communion] as a sharing and believe there will be an ever increasing understanding of what it means." And we are reminded by a North Carolinian, "Children learn by doing and experiencing." A layperson from Montana reports that "during an intergenerational Sunday evening informal worship, the previous pastor used communion participation as a 'learning tool,'" and adds, "In our formal church setting, this would not be appreciated by some members." A Kansas pastor states the case for communing children succinctly:

> We believe that when we come to the Lord's table as a family of faith that we can't tell the children that they can't eat with us. I believe that this is a learning experience when children begin to know Jesus through the elements and when they can begin to learn what it means to be a member of the church. We want to share Christ—so how can we limit with whom we share it [*communion*].

A Kentucky congregation has adopted a practice that not only allows for children's participation in the Lord's Supper in corporate worship but offers children's worship as well:

> Our children attend a children's worship experience outside of the sanctuary but join the adults during the hymn of invitation so that we may all receive communion together after the hymn.

3. **Parental guidance and conversation** is the most frequent and expected form of communion education either in expectation of receiving communion at some later time or participating in the present. Disciples do agree that preparation for communion is primarily the privilege and responsibility of parents before and whenever communion participation begins and continues and so an Alaskan pastor is encouraged to say, "Scripture does not speak to this issue [*whether to commune unbaptized children*], so parents should help educate a child as to the reason and importance of this sacred event. To do otherwise wouldn't be Disciple. Not only that, a Maryland layperson puts an additional responsibility on parents: "We are free to let the children partake with the hope that the parents will take responsibility to insure that participation is dignified and without disruption to the others around the table."

A Missouri layperson decries the lack of parental guidance: "I believe it's sacrilegious but parents obviously do not take communion emblems seriously. Perhaps parents have not been taught differently. It is probably a neglected area of teaching discipleship." An Indiana pastor concludes, "My main encouragement to parents is the importance of 'participating with understanding.'"

Having placed the burden of children's communion on parents it remains to see how much help they are getting from their church for this formidable task.

4. **Pastoral counseling and instruction** takes a variety of forms both personal and congregational as reported by pastors. Of those churches reporting who makes the decision to commune children, 10% said that it was a combination including parents and pastor. This strongly suggests an intentional collaboration (and, in some instances, conflict) between parents and pastors that must, at the very least, require conversation with some degree of counseling and instruction. Instruction regarding communion is typically a part of the pastor's class about which an Illinois pastor says, "In pastor's class we discover the real reasons and meanings of communion. Prior to that it is up to the parents." Several other instructional roles of the pastor are reported:

> If children indicate an interest in receiving communion the pastor talks with child and the parents and if it is determined that participation would be helpful to the child's faith development, they can then participate. The elders are informed. (Ohio pastor)

> About 30% of children participate. Children usually do not take communion because of lack of education of the families. [*It is more common for churches to report that children do commune because of a lack of education of the families.*] Parents in consultation with pastor make the final decision with the children, letting them know that Christ invites all. (Kentucky pastor)

> Periodically, I explain communion to our children in the regular Children's Sermon and allow them to taste the elements. Included in the homily is the promise that they can participate when they are baptized. This is a teaching experience for the entire congregation. However, we do not have a binding rule that children cannot participate, and occasionally parents feel that their children are ready and allow them to partake." (Georgia pastor)

> Sometimes I will have children commune who are not baptized to teach a lesson. I'm sure that some are appalled by this, but I am more interested in teaching about God than someone's rules. (Ohio pastor)

> Once every four years during the children's sermon I let the kids eat and drink the elements. I tell them that it does not taste all that good. Communion is for the time when you and your parents feel you really understand its meaning. (Illinois pastor)

> On World Communion Sunday I encouraged people to share and celebrate the Lord's Supper with our children (in my sermon). Since then, almost all our children now participate. (Illinois pastor)

> This issue is addressed in the Pastor's Welcome Class for new members and their families. They are told that the practice is discouraged and that this is an opportunity for families to talk about their faith. (Kansas pastor)

> I encourage parents to discuss the meaning of communion with their children and 1) be consistent with all their children, 2) make a family decision about participation without baptism, and 3) lean toward allowing participation once children can express an understanding that this is a special part of worship, not a snack. (Iowa pastor)

The pastor of a Dallas congregation returned with his survey an invitation to the Christmas Eve Family Service and a series of four articles he had written for his church newsletter on the subject of children and the Lord's Supper. The articles are thoughtfully written and make a strong case. In the last article he stated his own conclusions with supporting arguments that are well-stated but not included here:

> 1. I can find nothing in the New Testament which explicitly requires baptism for participation in the Lord's Supper.
> 2. The New Testament requires that those who participate in the service of the Lord's Supper be people of personal faith.
> 3. Understood Biblically, Baptism is supposed to be the initial response of personal faith an individual makes to the preaching of the Gospel.
> 4. If it is determined that a person possesses sufficient faith to participate in a service of the Lord's Supper, does not that person possess sufficient faith to be baptized?

This pastor's invitation to communion for the Christmas Eve Family Service puts into practice the beliefs that he has already communicated to the congregation:

> [*Name of church*] is a believers' church. We recognize the importance of each individual's decision of faith. We are not Christians because our parents were Christians. We are not Christians because our siblings are Christian. We are Christians because we have made the personal, conscious and deliberate decision to believe that Jesus Christ is the Son of God, to obey him as our Lord and to trust him as our Savior.
> Ordinarily, in the Christian Church, we would encourage people who have made this decision of faith to be baptized by immersion, and would then welcome them to the Lord's Super. But we are also a church which believes in the right of private interpretation and which urges a respectful tolerance of the faith and practices of others. In fact, we are a church which was born in the act of refusing to block the approach of people with different understandings of discipleship to participate in the service of the Lord's Table. We did not fence the table then. We do not fence the table now. The decision about who will participate in this

service is not ours to make. It is up to you. It is a question of your faith. And the question of whether or not your unbaptized children should participate in this service is not one we will decide for you either. We invite you to carefully reflect on the spiritual significance of the bread we break and the cup we bless, we expect you to make an informed decision, and then we will respect your practice even if it varies from our own.

If you make the decision that your unbaptized children will not take communion here this afternoon, this does not mean that they should not come forward. We have a Christmas gift from the church for every child here, and it will be given to them from up here. Also, we have a tray of fish shaped crackers for those children who are not ready for communion yet, but who nevertheless has some beginning awareness of the importance of Jesus Christ and who want a special way of celebrating the day he was born by doing something which imitates the faith of those who have already confessed him as Lord and received him as Savior. The fish shaped crackers are a wonderful way of witnessing to our kids about the importance of Jesus Christ to us because the letters forming the word "fish" in Greek are the first letters of the Greek words meaning, "Jesus Christ, Son of God, Savior." Because the fish has always been one of the basic signs of Christianity, we can use it here today as a sign of our faith to those who have not yet fully made it their own.

5. **Organized classes** and other special activities offer opportunities for churches to teach about the Lord's Supper. These include membership classes, junior church, Sunday school and other activities. A Virginia church, for example, uses a children's program during worship that includes a "feast," about which the pastor says, "The children learn symbolism and procedures." An adult membership class in Missouri has a session on the Lord's Supper that includes

Part II · There's Room at the Table

the reason for including children in communion. A North Carolina church has a novel approach:

> We have a special children's communion service after the children's sermon. It is conducted by a layman/S.S. teacher preceding their dismissal to their nursery. When they no longer go to Nursery (age 7) they remain in the sanctuary and communion with the adults. By that age they have memorized the words of institution and the special children's prayer.
>
> We offer annual instruction regarding the Lord's Supper. This event is open and attended by children and adults. (New York pastor)
>
> The children who attend Primary Worship receive teaching and training in the way of salvation, worship and church membership. Some of these children are baptized and others are unbaptized. By an informal agreement they all participate in the observance of the Lord's Supper. The observance of the Lord's Supper is supervised by the Elders. (North Carolina pastor)
>
> Up until grade 3 children go to children's worship so are not in the service at communion. We have begun a spring introduction to worship, baptism and communion for 2nd graders and their parents prior to the children's participation in the entire service. (New Mexico pastor)

Occasionally, congregations offer mentoring programs such as this one in Montana:

> Since we have young children in worship without parents on a somewhat regular basis, the Elders have agreed to watch for such situations, identify such children, sit with them during worship on a one-on-one basis, help them in a mentoring fashion to understand what is happening during worship including

helping them take communion (including what it means at an age appropriate level and teaching them to pray during such times).

Sometimes what happens in children's church is at odds with what the pastor teaches and practices as an Indiana pastor notes:

> I have just discovered this practice [*children's communion in children's church*] and don't agree our children "participate" as they commune in children's church. Since I am not present I cannot intervene yet.

6. **Written policies and directives** were offered by some churches. For example, a church in California offers a four-page guide to worship prepared by the elders to "simplify worship and make your visit with our Lord more meaningful." The guide contains a section on communion that includes the following instructions that leave no doubt regarding the requirements for children's communion in that congregation:

> CHILDREN'S PARTICIPATION
> IN COMMUNION SERVICES
>
> Children must be taught that they should:
> § Have reached the age of accountability (Usually no younger than 10)
> § Make public their confession of faith that they believe Jesus Christ is the Son of the Living God and that they take him as their personal savior
> § Be baptized for forgiveness of sins and receive the Holy Spirit
> § Lead a Christian lifestyle
> § Support the work of Christ with their presence, prayers, talents and service before they are ready to take communion.

It is common for churches to use a printed invitation that includes such phrases as "all baptized believers," "all who believe in Jesus Christ," "all Christians," "all believers," "all are welcome to the Lord's Table," etc. These are meant to clarify to whom the invitation is extended but are often ambiguous in regard to children. For example, can children be believers or Christian and are they included in "all" or is this qualified in some way? It might be noted that verbal invitations often have the same ambiguity. One statement that offers a clear choice is from a Kansas congregation's bulletin:

> Children are invited to receive the bread and wine if it is their parent's wish, or they may receive a blessing from the pastor or server, simply request this when you come forward.

Central Woodward Christian Church in Troy, Michigan has developed an excellent program to assist parents and children in worship and the Lord's Supper. The congregation made a decision to involve children in the entirety of worship for the following reasons:

> § CWCC is a church of inclusion, not exclusion.
> § This church has made a strong commitment to children in recent years.
> § Including children in the entirety of worship reinforces our commitment, as a church and as a denomination, to all members of our church family.
> § Including children in the entirety of worship reinforces to children Christ's message of the importance of children.
> § Including children in the entirety of worship provides children with important learning and worship opportunities (children cannot learn to worship unless they are a part of worship).

Children at the Lord's Table

Among other materials designed to help children gain the most from their worship experience are three printed pieces. The first is a children's book that is placed in the pews, "A Children's Guide to Worship," that contains a bookplate on the inside cover that includes this statement:

> We have the Lord's Supper every week when we worship. Your parents will tell you if you may or may not take the communion. Some families in our church want children to wait until they are baptized to eat and drink the communion, other families do not believe baptism is necessary before taking communion. In our church we respect each other's decisions on this matter.

The second piece of literature is a five-page pamphlet, "Children and Communion," that offers helpful suggestions to include children in communion and includes the following statement:

> The majority of the elders of Central Woodard Christian Church (Disciples of Christ) consider it appropriate for children to participate in communion, for many of the reasons cited in this pamphlet; however, an earnest minority believe otherwise.
> One of the hallmarks of the Christian Church (Disciples of Christ) is liberty in matters of faith and theology. When there is no clear consensus, after careful and prayerful consideration, it is our practice to respect each other's beliefs.
> In short, at Central Woodward Christian Church children who have not yet been baptized may or may not participate in communion depending upon their parent's prayerful decision on this matter. Parents should feel free to talk with the pastor or any of the elders regarding this decision.

The third piece is a tri-fold, "Parenting in the Pews," that offers parents helpful and practical advice in assisting children in worship.

A congregation in Oregon also offers a "Children in Worship" tri-fold as a guide for parents and the church when children are in worship that includes this statement:

> Communion is the highlight of worship and all are welcome to participate. You will want to talk with your children about the meaning of this important time. If your child is interested in participating, talk with them about its Spiritual meaning prior to participating.

The pastor adds, "We usually let the parents decide about the age to begin taking communion. There is some teaching and help for the parents so that they can decide when their children have a basic understanding of communion. We also talk about the Lord's Supper in our 3rd–5th grade youth group."

The elders of a Texas congregation approved a statement in 1987 regarding children in worship:

> We see participation in the weekly observance of communion as appropriately following the first two actions which have been taken by the believer [*confession of faith and baptism*]. Our denomination has understood communion as an "ordinance," that is, that it is an act of obedience and discipline which the Christian enters into in response to the invitation of our Lord and Savior, and to do so in memory of him.
>
> While no one among us would attempt to re-frame our history and tradition to suit ourselves, the above beliefs and traditions [*confession of faith and baptism precede communion*] continue to leave real questions and personal needs un-met in regard to our children's inclusion in the partaking of the communion elements. For example, ages vary from person to person when decision is made to publicly confess Jesus as Lord, and to submit to Christian baptism. In addition, younger children who are responding to their nurturing in significant and meaningful ways, cannot understand why they are not

> actively encouraged to partake of the communion emblems. In addition to teaching them in the home and in the church as to the reasons why we believe as we do, and in order to address these and other questions, we wish to affirm another principle long held dear in our tradition—that is, the freedom of the conscience (within the fellowship) in regard to the believer's worship, witness and theological formulation of the individual.
> This freedom of belief and expression is held dear. In this spirit of freedom, we believe that parents, with children who have not yet made public confession of faith nor been baptized, are free to make family decisions about those children partaking of the communion elements. We recommend that such times be limited to special services of the church year such as Christmas and Easter, and to other Sunday worship or special events when parents and their children worship together in church worship as a family group.
> We affirm that our beliefs and practices mentioned only briefly here are central to our witness as a people and need to be understood and valued. At the same time we affirm our need to be sensitive to the very young, to the very old and all those in the Christian Pilgrimage.

The narrative responses to the survey indicate that observation, participation and parental guidance and conversation are the principal means by which children are prepared for the Lord's Supper in Christian Churches (Disciples of Christ). However, because children are so seldom in worship during the time of communion this has serious limitations and communion in children's worship is not seen as "real" communion by many adults. Pastoral counseling and instruction is limited for the most part to pastor's classes and an occasional conversation with parents. Organized classes for children often address the subject but too often long after the "teachable moment" has passed.

Written directives, policies and supporting materials for children and parents have been prepared by a small minority of congregations some of which are quite good. Because the decision regarding their children's communion is primarily a parental task more supporting materials would be welcomed by parents facing this important decision and educational responsibility.

✢ ✢ ✢

Unintended Consequence of the Survey

The small space for comments on the survey was intended to allow people to express additional comments and explanations, a simple courtesy for those who might have something they wished to share. They did this far beyond our expectation and in detail that was nothing short of amazing. Some of the life experiences were so passionate and detailed that they could not be quoted for fear of embarrassing or harming the writer. Some begged for help and some said it would only stir up trouble in their congregations. Some congregations called meetings of their elders who decided to study the matter and some voted not to respond to the survey but let the surveyor know that it was none of his business. Some were carefully written statements supporting a particular view or describing the problem. Some criticized the survey itself or the right of the surveyor to ask the questions. But most agreed that it is an extremely important issue among Disciples. **A major result of the survey is that**

it suggests a need for a process of discernment among Disciples of Christ.

The design of the survey was intended to be short, straightforward and unambiguous with a few questions that could be answered "yes" or "no." This would assure a greater response that, we believe, has indeed happened. Many people, however, found the first question difficult to answer not because they couldn't look at the congregation and see whether unbaptized children were receiving communion or not receiving communion but because they wanted to explain their answer with a "yes, but" or a "no, but" or even a "yes and no." The result of this reluctance to be pinned down to a simple 'yes" or "no," as you may have recognized in some of the quotes previously cited, partially explains the amazing number of narrative responses of which we have seen a small sampling

The idea of unintended consequences was amply illustrated in the responses to the survey. In fact, the serendipitous consequence of this survey is a vivid portrait of children and the Lord's Supper in our churches. It is of much greater use and interest than the bare statistics that show us the extent of the picture without its color and composition. That this picture was created by the respondents voluntarily and without the urging of the surveyor adds validity to the comments. The pastors and lay people wanted to be heard!

The insistence that their answers to the first question be qualified by narrative answers revealed that our congregations have a tremendous diversity in the matter of communing children Children's participation in communion has been placed on a continuum to illustrate the variety of practices. The continuum is from "all unbaptized children receive communion" to "no unbaptized children receive communion." It is not an exhaustive list because our churches have an amazing capacity to adapt their practices to their particular beliefs and understandings and to seek compromises to accommodate different opinions. It is more a generosity of spirit than a narrowness of mind.

Continuum of Children's Communion Participation in the Christian Church (Disciples of Christ)

Unbaptized children are never served communion.

Baptized children from other faith groups who have not made their confession of faith (confirmed) are never served communion.

Invitation for communion is for persons who have confessed their faith and been baptized regardless of age.

Unbaptized children who attempt to participate in communion are publicly reprimanded (usually by a parent).

An elder or the pastor talks privately to the parents of unbaptized children who participate in communion explaining that communion should come after baptism.

Congregation includes children in communion by offering them a blessing.

Congregation includes children in communion by

substituting raisins, grapes, fish crackers or cheerios for the bread and wine of communion.

Congregation basically believes that participation in communion should follow confession of faith and baptism but allows freedom to participate to the few parents and children who wish to do so, especially those from other faith traditions.

Congregation basically believes that participation in communion should follow confession of faith and baptism but allows children to participate in communion in children's worship or an extended church school session which some describe as a *feast*.

Congregation basically believes that participation in communion should follow confession of faith and baptism but allows children to participate on special days such as Christmas Eve and Maundy Thursday or in special services such as contemporary worship, family camp worship, etc.

Congregation basically believes that participation in communion should follow confession of faith and baptism but ignores the communion of children by those who disagree.

Congregation takes no position for or against children's communion.

Congregation allows children to commune before baptism but expect a certain level of understanding that the congregation determines.

Congregation asserts the right of parents to make this decision and supports equally those who wish their children to have their first communion after baptism and those who choose to commune their children before baptism as a part of the family of God.

Congregation embraces children as a part of the family of God and invites all children to the fellowship of the table. The parents, along with the child, decide when the child is ready to accept the invitation. Often, pastors and elders are mentors in helping the parents make this decision.

✣ ✣ ✣

There's Room at the Table

The end of World War II brought with it many changes in American life including an increased interest in church attendance and an optimistic belief that the American family and American mainline churches could together create a grand and glorious future for the American family in a postwar world. At the middle of the 20th Century, education was booming in both the secular and sacred spheres, churches were growing, and families were increasing in size following the delay of a long war and an increasing prosperity making it possible for more families to rear children in a secure environment. Rightly or wrongly, we considered ourselves to be a child-centered culture and set about the task of rethinking childhood.

With this burgeoning interest in children, a movement among those new families and a society that favored them began to increase children's participation in worship with family worship services becoming popular much as contemporary worship today. And what greater potential for participation was there than the drama of the Lord's Supper at the center of our worship! It was inevitable that some would take issue with the exclusion of children from the Lord's Supper making this a live issue for the past half-century. This movement has gained momentum with passionate argument on both sides of the issue whether children who are baptized but not confirmed or children who have not been baptized should share in this sacred meal. This movement has progressed surely and persistently across denominational lines and continues to this day, asking the question, "Is there room at the Table for children?"

A reading of ecclesiastical history reminds us that this is a question that the church began asking early in its history. In the author's historical study of the role of the child in the Lord's Supper, we have a documented account of the church's struggle with finding and maintaining a place at the Table for children. The conclusion to which that study led was this:

The communion of children was the general practice of Christendom for its first millennium with the Eastern Church never departing from the practice to this day. The Western Church began to withdraw communion from young children for theological reasons, primarily the doctrine of *the real presence* because it was difficult to commune young children with the wine as had been the custom. At the beginning of the Protestant Reformation in the 16th Century, the Roman Catholic Church decreed that communion was not necessary for salvation before *the years of discretion* and Protestant churches moved toward the same position relating first communion to confirmation although there were many exceptions and much disagreement. The gradual recovery of children's participation in the Lord's Supper began in the mid twentieth century and continues to this day in much of Western Christendom, a recovery in which the Christian Church (Disciples of Christ) is taking an active role.

The movie rating system in use for rating the appropriateness of movies for children and adolescents by American standards can, interestingly enough, be used to describe the church's attitude toward the communion of children at different times and places and for various parts of the church universal during its long history and during the shorter history of the Christian Church (Disciples of Christ).

For Disciples, the **G (General Audiences)** rating is used by some congregations that practice children's communion in such settings as children's church with or without parental guidance and in churches where the invitation to the Table in corporate worship specifically invites children.

The **PG (Parental Guidance Suggested)** rating is increasingly becoming the norm for our congregations with parents being given the final word as to when and if their children will be communed.

The **PG-13 (Parents Strongly Cautioned)** rating expresses the desire that children who commune have reached the age of accountability as shown by their confession of faith and baptism or have an *understanding* of the Lord's Supper. However, the final decision is left to the parents who are "strongly cautioned." Understanding comes at an earlier age than accountability so it is much younger with a third of our churches that commune unbaptized children first doing so between the ages of six and eight and one-third between the ages of three and five. One-fifth of those churches use a far less cognitive meaning of understanding and commune children between birth and two.

The **R (Restricted)** rating requires children under 17 to be accompanied by a parent or adult guardian. For Disciples this rating would suggest that children who have not been baptized would not be served communion unless they are accompanied by a parent or other responsible adult who permits it.

The new **NC-17 (no one 17 and under admitted)** rating which replaces the old **X (minors not admitted)** rating would apply to those churches that do not allow any unbaptized child to commune. The age could be changed by the congregation to accommodate the age at which baptism occurs. It could be **NC-8, NC-12,** etc.

It might be helpful to new people with children visiting our churches to have the communion rating published alongside the listing of the communion service in the worship bulletin. But whatever rating is given the Lord's Supper for the guidance of children's participation, it must be done with an understanding of its objective meaning (theology), its consequence for the participants both individually and collectively (pastoral concern), and its subjective significance for the communicant (faith and psychology).

This survey of Christian Church (Disciples of Christ) congregations indicates that although congregations may offer a variety of ratings for their observance of the Lord's Supper, there is a serious effort in each of them to find ways in which children may come to know Jesus in response to his command, "Let the children come to me." Congregations are struggling to find ways to be welcoming to children while being faithful to theological convictions and the personal sensitivities of children and adults alike. While it would appear that communing children is rapidly becoming a parental decision that is not only allowed but encouraged in many of our churches, other congregations feel just as strongly that children should be baptized before their first communion. There is a widespread uncertainty in still other congregations with an ambivalence regarding when and if these children should be communed and what level of understanding is necessary. It is also clear that many congregations are asking for help in making this difficult decision. The survey elicited conversations in many congregations and some of these congregations were even prompted to have official discussions in elders meetings and other groups.

In conclusion

The Christian Church (Disciples of Christ) is moving to an earlier age for first communion with the necessity of baptism before communion being increasingly challenged. Congregations and pastors who have hesitated to discuss this "touchy" issue are engaging in more frank and open discussion. Parents are being given more and more authority in making the decision regarding their child's first communion. And finally, in keeping with Disciples tradition, churches are finding creative and sensitive ways to find room at the Table for children without violating the theological convictions or pastoral concerns of their constituency. In all of this we are continuing to embrace our diversity as we bend to the promptings of the Holy Spirit who seeks to make us one at the table of our Lord.

Appendix 1

A Survey of the Christian Church (Disciples of Christ) Concerning
The Role of the Child in the Observance of the Lord's Supper

1. Do children in your congregation take communion prior to baptism? ☐ Yes ☐ No

2. Does your congregation have a common understanding or informal agreement on children's participation in the Lord's Supper? ☐ Yes ☐ No

   If yes, does it suggest ☐ participation or ☐ non-participation?

3. Does your congregation have a formal policy regarding children's participation in the Lord's Supper? ☐ Yes ☐ No

   If yes, does it provide for ☐ participation or ☐ non-participation?

4. If unbaptized children commune, at what age do they begin _____, and who makes the decision?

   ☐ Parents ☐ Pastor ☐ Elders ☐ Others _____

5. Comments which you would like to share:

Name of person answering questionnaire: _____
☐ Clergy ☐ Lay Leader

Church: _____

Address: _____

Phone: (___) _____   e-mail: _____

Please Return to: John T. Hinant
5455 Younkin Drive
Indianapolis IN 46268

Appendix 2

		#1			#2				#3				#4					# resp.
	lay	cler	yes	no	both	yes	no	par	non	yes	no	par	non	age	Par	Pas	Eld	oth	
Alabama	1	17	11	4	3	12	6	4	6	2	15		1		12				18
Alaska		1	1			1		1											1
Arizona	1	9	5	2	2	8	1	5	3	1	8	1	1	1	7	2			11
Arkansas	4	25	12	10	5	21	8	8	10	1	26	1	0		17	1		1	30
California	9	85	64	34	5	74	21	43	18	8	85	3	4		77	13	5		98
Colorado	3	24	22	2	2	19	7	9	5	4	20	3	0		19	4	3		27
Connecticut		1	1				1				1				1				1
Dist. of Columbia		2	1	1		2			1		2				2				2
Florida	4	36	17	17	3	30	10	9	19	2	39	2	1		29	5	4		41
Georgia	2	24	18	11		17	11	5	10	4	24	1	3		15	1			33
Hawaii		1	1			1		1			1								1
Idaho		5	5		1	6	1	4	1		7				5				6
Illinois	11	75	40	27	19	59	28	16	39	4	81	2	2		69	8			89
Indiana	29	120	78	60	7	109	35	41	66	7	134	2	5		104	14	4		147
Iowa	7	72	36	30	12	46	27	13	27	3	71	0	2		55	6		3	80
Kansas	8	62	36	24	10	46	23	17	24	2	66	1	2		51	6	3	1	70
Kentucky	16	80	44	44	8	65	34	13	47	3	93	3	3		56	6	1		99
Louisiana		7	3	2	2	7	0	2	3		7				5				7
Maryland	4	12	8	4	4	13	2	6	6	2	12		1		11	1	1		16
Massachusetts	1	1	1	1		2		1	1		2				1	1	1		2
Michigan	5	20	16	4	3	13	10	4	4	2	21		1		15	4	1		25
Minnesota	1	5	2	3	1	6		4	2						4	3			6

	#1					#2					#3				#4				# resp.
Mississippi	28	1																	1
Missouri	122	64	71	17	112	1	41	29	80	1	149	3	2	1	85	6	2	3	155
Montana	7	8		4	8		4	5	2		10	1	1	1	8	2			12
Nebraska	21	10	17	3	22		8	6	11		25	2	0	1	19	2			30
Nevada	1			1			1				1				1				1
														6-7					
New Mexico	9	4	2	3	6		3	2	2		9	0	0	0	9		1		9
New York	17	11	8	4	22		1	13	8		19	3	2	1	15				23
North Carolina	54	43	20	3	37		29	17	19		59	6	0	6	46	7	2	2	66
Ohio	75	35	43	12	63		26	17	45		78	10	4	6	55	13	4	3	91
Oklahoma	66	36	24	16	45		30	15	27		74	2		2	53	3	1	3	76
Oregon	20	15	2	9	18		8	8	7		25				20	3	2	1	26
Pennsylvania	23	16	10	5	21		10	10	11		30	2	1		22	4			32
South Carolina	9	5	4	1	8		2	5	2		5	3	1	2	7	3			10
South Dakota		4			4		4		3			1	4				3		4
Tennessee	20	10	8	10	18		10	5	10		27	1	1		20	1			35
Texas	158	105	60	18	119		59	40	69		159	13	8	6	125	12	5	5	183
Utah	1	1			1		1	1	1		1				1				1
Virginia	63	44	40	3	61		30	16	34		82	4	2	2	55	4	1		92
Washington	32	23	10	7	30		10	18	7		35	2		1	31	4			42
West Virginia	17	4	7	10	15		7	3	11		21			1	14				22
Wisconsin	2	2					2		1		2				2				2
Wyoming	3	2		1	2			2			3				2	1	1		3
Canada	8	3	4	4	8		3	3	5		7	2	1		6				11
TOTAL	262 1,413	867	611	218	1,178		513	421	647	100	1,537		41	56	1,152	139	44	23	1,737

Appendix 3

2000/2001 Survey of the Christian Church (Disciples of Christ)
Concerning
The Role of the Child in the Observance of the Lord's Supper

Survey Statistics by Question

	number	actual %	rounded to nearest whole %
Total Responses:	1,737		
Total Questionnaires mailed:	3,770		
Percent who responded:		46.1 %	46 %
Respondents:			
Lay	262	15.6 %	
Clergy	1,413	84.4 %	
Total who indicated clergy or lay	1,675		

1. Do children in your congregation take communion prior to baptism?

Yes	867	51.1 %	
Checked both yes and no	218	12.9 %	
Percent of positive replies			64 %
(checked either *yes* or both *yes* and *no*)			
No	611	36.0%	36 %
Total who responded to this question 1,696			

2. Does your congregation have a common understanding or informal agreement on children's participation in the Lord's Supper?

Yes	1178	69.6 %	70 %
No	514	30.4 %	30 %
If yes, does it suggest participation or non-participation?			
Participation	421	39.2 %	39 %
Non-Participation	647	60.8 %	61 %

3. Does your congregation have a formal policy regarding children's participation in the Lord's Supper?

Yes	100	6.1 %	6 %
No	1543	93.9 %	94 %
If yes, does it provide for participation or non-participation?			
Participation	41	41.8 %	42 %
Non-participation	56	58.2 %	58 %

4. If unbaptized children commune, at what age do they begin and who makes the decision, parents, pastor, elders, others?
(Percentage based on total responses)

Parents	1152	66.3 %	66 %
Clergy	139	8.0 %	8 %
Elders	44	2.5 %	3 %
Others	23	1.3 %	1 %

If unbaptized children commune, at what age do they begin and who makes the decision....?

370 persons responded to the first part of this question regarding the age at which unbaptized children begin communion. 339 gave a specific age or a range of ages and 31 gave narrative responses. 17 of the latter were age suggestive, 6 were school grade specific and 8 were non-age specific.

Age at which unbaptized children begin communion

Age	Number	Age	Number
Any age	32	6-12	1
Birth	3	7	21
6 mos.	1	7-8	12
1	19	7-9	3
2	9	7-10	2
2-3	6	8	19
3	11	8-9	13
3-4	8	8-10	13
3-5	2	8-12	1
3-7	1	9	1
4	8	9-10	10
4-5	13	9-12	1
4-6	2	10	10
4-7	1	10-11	2
5	21	10-12	3
5-6	18	10-13	1
5-7	7	11	1
5-8	2	12	11
5-10	1	12-14	1
6	25	12-15	1
6-7	7	13	2
6-8	9	14	1
6-10	2		

Grouping these ages we have the following number of responses and percentage of the total responses:

Birth-2	70	19 %
3-5 95	95	26 %
6-8	129	35 %
9-15	45	12 %

Dividing the 31 narrative responses into three categories provided the following criteria:

Non-age specific responses
5—Age varies
1—When parents allow it
1—When parents think child is old enough
1—When parents believe it is necessary

School grade specific
3—Pre-school
1—Kindergarten
1—Early elementary
1—Grade school

Age suggestive
4—When they ask or show interest
2—As soon as they can walk down the aisle and participate
1—As early as they can grab the bread
2—As soon as they are able
1—As soon as they desire to do so
5—Early and as young as possible
1—Right away

Adding the school grades and suggestive age according to the behavior of the child to the age groupings changes the numbers and percentages slightly as follows:

Birth – 2	80	22 %
3 – 5	111	30 %
6 – 8	129	35 %
9 – 15	42	12 %
Other criteria	8	8 %

Persons who make the decision to commune unbaptized children

Who makes the decision regarding the communing of unbaptized children resulted in an overwhelming affirmation of parental rights in this matter when compared to pastors and elders. Most of those who checked others referred to the children themselves who, of course, have a natural choice in the matter. Some referred to grandparents who often bring grandchildren to church. And a few referred to the church as making the decision.

Parents (alone)	1035	87.8 %
Clergy (alone)	18	1.5 %
Elders (alone)	5	.4 %
Parents/Clergy	87	7.4 %
Parents/Elders	2	.2 %
Parents/Clergy/Elders	30	2.6 %
Clergy/Elders	2	.2 %
Total	1179	
Parents alone and with others	1154	97.9 %

Source Notes

Part I: Finding a Place at the Table
The Child's Life in the Cradle of Christianity

1. William Barclay, *Train Up a Child, Educational Ideals in the Ancient World* (Philadelphia, The Westminster Press, 1959), p. 11.

2. A. C. Bouquet, *Everyday Life in Bible Times*, cited by William Barclay, p. 14.

3. William Barclay, *Train Up a Child, Educational Ideals in the Ancient World*, pp. 14, 22-23, 27.

Children in the Church of the Apostles

1. William Barclay, *Train Up a Child, Educational Ideals in the Ancient World*, p 11,

2. S. Schechter, *Studies in Judaism, First Series*, p.300, quoted by William Barclay *Train Up a Child, Educational Ideals in the Ancient World*, p. 35.

3. Hans Lietzmann, *The Beginnings of the Christian Church*, translated by Bertram Woolf, (New York, Charles Scribners' Sons, 1937), pp. 78-79 and Phillip Schaff, *History of the Apostolic Church with a General Introduction to Church History*, translated by Edw. Yeomans, (New York, Charles Scribners' Co., 1870), p. 546.

4. W. D. Davies, *Christian Origins and Judaism*, (Philadelphia, The Westminster Press, 1962), p. 217.

5. *Hans Lietzmann, The Beginnings of the Christian Church*, translated by Bertram Woolf, (New York, Charles Scribners' Sons, 1937), p253.

6. Hans Lietzmann, *The Beginnings of the Christian Church*, translated by Bertram Woolf, (New York, Charles Scribners' Sons, 1937), p. 243.

Children in the Church Coming of Age

1. James Donaldson and Alexander Robert, editors, *Ante-Nicene Christian Library, Vol. V*, (Edinburgh, T & T Clark, 1868-1873, republished by Wm. B. Erdman's Publishing Co, 1957, Grand Rapids, Michigan), 258.

Source Notes

2. Cyprian, *De Lapsis* quoted by William Wall, *The History of Infant Baptism, Vol. I*, (Oxford, University Pres, 1862), p. 631.

3. James Donaldson and Alexander Robert, editors, *Ante-Nicene Christian Library, Vol V*, (Edinburgh, T &T Clark, 1868-1873, republished by Wm. B. Erdman's Publishing Co., 1957), pp.353-4.

4. R. Hugh Connolly, "Introduction and Notes," *Didiscalia Apostolorum, the Syriac Version Translated and Accompanied by the Verona Latin Fragments*, (Oxford, Clarendon Press, 1929, lithographed edition, Norwich, Fletcher and Son, Ltd., 1969) p. 120.

5. James Donaldson and Alexander Robert, editors, *Ante-Nicene Christian Library, Vol. VII*, (Edinburgh, T & T Clark, 1868-1873, republished by Wm. B. Erdman's Publishing Co., 1957), pp 483-491.

6. John Meyendorf, excerpted from a personal letter, November 30, 1967.

7. Wm. J. McDonald, editor-in-chief, *New Catholic Encyclopedia, Vol. IV*, (New York, McGraw Hill, 1967), p. 37 and Helmut T. Lehman, editor, *Meaning and Practice of the Lord's Supper*, (Philadelphia, Muhlenberg Press, 1961), pp. 83-84.

Children's Communion in a Favored Church

1. Philip Schaff, *History of the Christian Church, Vol. II* (Grand Rapids, Michigan, Wm. B. Eerdmans Publishing Co, 1910), pp. 66-72.

2. Philip Schaff, *History of the Christian Church, Vol. II* (Grand Rapids, Michigan, Wm. B. Eerdmans Publishing Co, 1910), p. 72.

3. Joachim Jeremias, *Infant Baptism in the First Four Centuries*, translated by David Cairns, (London, SCM Press, 1960), p. 92.

4. Joachim Jeremias, *Infant Baptism in the First Four Centuries*, translated by David Cairns, (London, SCM Pres, 1960), p. 90.

5. J. G. Davies, *Social Life of Early Christians*, (Boston, Little, Brown and Co., 1953),121.

Source Notes

6. J. G. Davies, *Social Life of Early Christians*, (Boston, Little, Brown and Co., 1953), 121.

7. Archdale A. King, *Eucharistic Reservation in the Western Church*, (New York, Sheed and Ward, 1964),

8. J. G. Davies, *Social Life of Early Christians*, (Boston, Little, Brown and Co, 1953), 97.

9. J. Clement Bennington, *The Recipient of Confirmation, A Historical Synopsis and Commentary*, (Washington, D.C., The Catholic University of America Press, 1952), p. 18.

10. Chrysostom, *Homily on John x*, cited by Lyman Coleman, *Ancient Christianity Exemplified in the Private, Domestic, and Civil Life of the Primitive Christians, and in the Original Institutions, Offices, Ordinances, and Rites of the Church*, (Philadelphia, J. B. Lippincott and Co., 1856), p. 65.

11. Chrysostom, *On Vain Glory and the Right Way for Parents to Bring up Their Children*, cited by William Barclay, *Train Up a Child, Educational Ideals in the Ancient World*, (Philadelphia, The Westminster Press, 1959), p. 16.

12. Lyman Coleman, *Ancient Christianity Exemplified in the Private, Domestic, and Civil Life of the Primitive Christians, and in the Original Institutions, Offices, Ordinances, and Rites of the Church*, (Philadelphia, J. B. Lippincott and Co., 1856), p. 431-2.

13. Augustine, *Sermon 174, Section 7*, cited by John T. Christian, *Close Communion: or, Baptism as a Prerequisite to the Lord's Supper*, (Louisville, Baptist Book Concern, 1892), p. 217.

14. W. H. Freestone, *The Sacrament Reserved, A Survey of the Practice of Reserving the Eucharist, with Special Reference to the Communion of the Sick, During the First Twelve Centuries*, (London, A. R. Mowbray and Milwaukee, The Young Churchman Co., 1917), pp. 176-7.

15. Gregory Dix, *The Shape of the Liturgy*, (Glasgow, University Press, 1945), p. 18.

16. Philip Schaff, *History of the Christian Church, Vol. III*, (New York, Charles Scribners' Sons, 1886), p. 492.

17. Philip Schaff, *History of the Christian Church, Vol. III*, (New York, Charles Scribners' Sons, 1886), p. 483.

Source Notes

18, L'Arroque, *The History of the Eucharist*, translated by Joseph Walker, (London, George Downes at the Three Flower de Luces, 1684), p. 127.

19. J. Clement Bennington, *The Recipient of Confirmation, A Historical Synopsis and Commentary*, (Washington, D.C., The Catholic University of America Press, 1952), p. 6.

20. W. E. Scudamore, *Notitia Eucharistica*, (London, Rivingtons, 1872), p. 49 citing *Metrophanis Crit. Confessio*, c. ix, p. 125.

21. W. E. Scudamore, *Notitia Eucharistica*, (London, Rivingtons, 1872), p. 49 citing *De Eccles. Dogm.* c. xxii. vii.

22. John T. Christian, *Close Communion: or, Baptism as a Prerequisite to the Lord's Supper*, (Louisville, Baptist Book Concern, 1892), p. 216.

23. W. H. Freestone, *The Sacrament Reserved, A Survey of the Practice of Reserving the Eucharist, with Special Reference to the Communion of the Sick, During the First Twelve Centuries*, (London, A. R. Mowbray and Milwaukee, (The Young Churchman Co., 1917), p. 177.

24. John T. Christian, *Close Communion: or, Baptism as a Prerequisite to the Lord's Supper*, (Louisville, Baptist Book Concern, 1892), p. 217.

25. John T. Christian, *Close Communion: or, Baptism as a Prerequisite to the Lord's Supper*, (Louisville, Baptist Book Concern, 1892), p. 170. See also Gregory Dix, *The Shape of the Liturgy*, (Glasgow, University Press, 1945), p. 123.

26. J. Clement Bennington, *The Recipient of Confirmation, A Historical Synopsis and Commentary*, (Washington, D.C., The Catholic University of America Press, 1952), p. 6.

27. W. H. Freestone, *The Sacrament Reserved, A Survey of the Practice of Reserving the Eucharist, with Special Reference to the Communion of the Sick, During the First Twelve Centuries*, (London, A. R. Mowbray and Milwaukee, (The Young Churchman Co., 1917), p. 177.

28. W. E. Scudamore, *Notitia Eucharistica*, (London, Rivingtons, 1872), p. 49 citing *The Gregorian Sacramentary*.

Source Notes

29. L'Arroque, *The History of the Eucharist*, translated by Joseph Walker, (London, George Downes at the Three Flower de Luces, 1684), p. 128.

30. John T. Christian, *Close Communion: or, Baptism as a Prerequisite to the Lord's Supper*, (Louisville, Baptist Book Concern, 1892), p. 217.

31. Oswald Reichel, *A Complete Manual of Canon Law, Vol. I, The Sacraments*. (London, John Hodges, 1896), 128.

32. L'Arroque, *The History of the Eucharist*, translated by Joseph Walker, (London, George Downes at the Three Flower de Luces, 1684), p. 128.

33. W. H. Freestone, *The Sacrament Reserved, A Survey of the Practice of Reserving the Eucharist, with Special Reference to the Communion of the Sick, During the First Twelve Centuries*, (London, A. R. Mowbray and Milwaukee, (The Young Churchman Co., 1917), p. 177.

34. T. E. Bridgett, *History of the Holy Eucharist in Great Britain, Vol. I,*. (London, C. Kegan Paul and Co., 1881), 221.

35. Oswald Reichel, *A Complete Manual of Canon Law, Vol. I, The Sacraments*. (London, John Hodges, 1896), 124.

36. T. E. Bridgett, *History of the Holy Eucharist in Great Britain, Vol. I,*. (London, C. Kegan Paul and Co., 1881), p. 221.

37. Boniface Luykx, "Confirmation in Relation to the Eucharist," *Readings in Sacramental Theology*, edited by C. Stephen Sullivan (Englewood Cliffs, New Jersey, Prentice-Hall, 1964). P. 200.

38. W. E. Scudamore, *Notitia Eucharistica*, (London, Rivingtons, 1872), p. 49 citing *The Gregorian Sacramentary*.

39, L'Arroque, *The History of the Eucharist*, translated by Joseph Walker, (London, George Downes at the Three Flower de Luces, 1684), p. 129.

40. W. H. Freestone, *The Sacrament Reserved, A Survey of the Practice of Reserving the Eucharist, with Special Reference to the Communion of the Sick, During the First Twelve Centuries*, (London, A. R. Mowbray and Milwaukee, (The Young Churchman Co., 1917), p. 250.

Source Notes

41. L'Arroque, *The History of the Eucharist*, translated by Joseph Walker, (London, George Downes at the Three Flower de Luces, 1684), p. 128.

42. L'Arroque, *The History of the Eucharist*, translated by Joseph Walker, (London, George Downes at the Three Flower de Luces, 1684), p. 128.

43. Lyman Coleman, *Ancient Christianity Exemplified in the Private, Domestic, and Civil Life of the Primitive Christians, and in the Original Institutions, Offices, Ordinances, and Rites of the Church*, (Philadelphia, J. B. Lippincott and Co., 1856), p. 432.

44. Boniface Luykx, "Confirmation in Relation to the Eucharist," *Readings in Sacramental Theology*, edited by C. Stephen Sullivan (Englewood Cliffs, New Jersey, Prentice-Hall, 1964), p. 199.

45. T. E. Bridgett, *History of the Holy Eucharist in Great Britain, Vol. I*,. (London, C. Kegan Paul and Co., 1881), p. 223.

46. L'Arroque, *The History of the Eucharist*, translated by Joseph Walker, (London, George Downes at the Three Flower de Luces, 1684), p. 128-129.

47. Boniface Luykx, "Confirmation in Relation to the Eucharist," *Readings in Sacramental Theology*, edited by C. Stephen Sullivan (Englewood Cliffs, New Jersey, Prentice-Hall, 1964), p. 198-9.

48. T. E. Bridgett, *History of the Holy Eucharist in Great Britain, Vol. II*,. (London, C. Kegan Paul and Co., 1881), p. 24.

49. John T. Christian, *Close Communion: or, Baptism as a Prerequisite to the Lord's Supper*, (Louisville, Baptist Book Concern, 1892), p. 218.

50. W. E. Scudamore, *Notitia Eucharistica*, (London, Rivingtons, 1872), p. 49.

51. J. D. C. Fisher, *Christian Initiation: Baptism in the Medieval West: A Study in the Disintegration of the Primitive Rite of Initiation*, (London, SPCK, 1965), p. 102.

52. Oswald Reichel, *A Complete Manual of Canon Law, Vol. I, The Sacraments*. (London, John Hodges, 1896), p. 128.

53. W. E. Scudamore, *Notitia Eucharistica*, (London, Rivingtons, 1872), p.50.

Source Notes

54. J. D. C. Fisher, *Christian Initiation: Baptism in the Medieval West: A Study in the Disintegration of the Primitive Rite of Initiation*, (London, SPCK, 1965), p. 102.

55. J. D. C. Fisher, *Christian Initiation: Baptism in the Medieval West: A Study in the Disintegration of the Primitive Rite of Initiation*, (London, SPCK, 1965), p. 102.

56. T. E. Bridgett, *History of the Holy Eucharist in Great Britain, Vol. II,*. (London, C. Kegan Paul and Co., 1881), p. 23.

57. T. E. Bridgett, *History of the Holy Eucharist in Great Britain, Vol. II,*. (London, C. Kegan Paul and Co., 1881), p. 24.

58. L'Arroque, *The History of the Eucharist*, translated by Joseph Walker, (London, George Downes at the Three Flower de Luces, 1684), p. 129,

59. Augustus Neander, *General History of the Christian Religion and Church, Vol. IV*, (Boston, Houghton, Mifflin and Co., 1871, 14th American edition), p. 341.

60. J. D. C. Fisher, *Christian Initiation: Baptism in the Medieval West: A Study in the Disintegration of the Primitive Rite of Initiation*, (London, SPCK, 1965), p. 104.

61. J. D. C. Fisher, *Christian Initiation: Baptism in the Medieval West: A Study in the Disintegration of the Primitive Rite of Initiation*, (London, SPCK, 1965), p. 103.

62. J. D. C. Fisher, *Christian Initiation: Baptism in the Medieval West: A Study in the Disintegration of the Primitive Rite of Initiation*, (London, SPCK, 1965), p. 103.

63. J. D. C. Fisher, *Christian Initiation: Baptism in the Medieval West: A Study in the Disintegration of the Primitive Rite of Initiation*, (London, SPCK, 1965), p. 102.

64. J. D. C. Fisher, *Christian Initiation: Baptism in the Medieval West: A Study in the Disintegration of the Primitive Rite of Initiation*, (London, SPCK, 1965), p. 103.

65. J. D. C. Fisher, *Christian Initiation: Baptism in the Medieval West: A Study in the Disintegration of the Primitive Rite of Initiation*, (London, SPCK, 1965), p. 105. [Note: Schaff gives the date as 1175 in *History of the Christian Church, Vol. V*, p. 724].

Source Notes

66. W. E. Scudamore, *Notitia Eucharistica*, (London, Rivingtons, 1872), p.50. [Note: It would appear likely that these three dates are confused and all refer to the same event.]

67. J. D. C. Fisher, *Christian Initiation: Baptism in the Medieval West: A Study in the Disintegration of the Primitive Rite of Initiation*, (London, SPCK, 1965), p. 104.

68. Philip Schaff, *History of the Christian Church, Vol. V Part I* (New York, Charles Scribners' Sons, 1886), p, 724 and J. D. C. Fisher, *Christian Initiation: Baptism in the Medieval West: A Study in the Disintegration of the Primitive Rite of Initiation*, (London, SPCK, 1965), p. 105.

69. J. D. C. Fisher, *Christian Initiation: Baptism in the Medieval West: A Study in the Disintegration of the Primitive Rite of Initiation*, (London, SPCK, 1965), p. 105.

70. Cyril E. Pocknee, *The Rites of Christian Initiation, Their Revision and Reform*, (London, A. J. Mowbray and Co., 1962), pp. 14-15.

71. T. E. Bridgett, *History of the Holy Eucharist in Great Britain, Vol. II,*. (London, C. Kegan Paul and Co., 1881), p. 25 and Oswald Reichel, *A Complete Manual of Canon Law, Vol. I, The Sacraments*. (London, John Hodges, 1896), p. 124.

72. J. D. C. Fisher, *Christian Initiation: Baptism in the Medieval West: A Study in the Disintegration of the Primitive Rite of Initiation*, (London, SPCK, 1965), p. 105.

73. T. E. Bridgett, *History of the Holy Eucharist in Great Britain, Vol. II,*. (London, C. Kegan Paul and Co., 1881), p. 25.

74. Philip Schaff, *History of the Christian Church, Vol. V Part I* (New York, Charles Scribners' Sons, 1886), p. 724.

75. Philip Schaff, *History of the Christian Church, Vol. V Part I* (New York, Charles Scribners' Sons, 1886), p. 724.

76. J. D. C. Fisher, *Christian Initiation: Baptism in the Medieval West: A Study in the Disintegration of the Primitive Rite of Initiation*, (London, SPCK, 1965), p. 105.

77. J. Clement Bennington, *The Recipient of Confirmation, A Historical Synopsis and Commentary*, (Washington, D.C., The Catholic University of America Press, 1952), p. 20.

Source Notes

78. Urban T. Holmes, *Young Children and the Eucharist*, (New York, The Seabury Press, 1972), p. 61.

79. J. D. C. Fisher, *Christian Initiation: Baptism in the Medieval West: A Study in the Disintegration of the Primitive Rite of Initiation*, (London, SPCK, 1965), p. 105.

80. J. D. C. Fisher, *Christian Initiation: Baptism in the Medieval West: A Study in the Disintegration of the Primitive Rite of Initiation*, (London, SPCK, 1965), p. 105.

81. J. D. C. Fisher, *Christian Initiation: Baptism in the Medieval West: A Study in the Disintegration of the Primitive Rite of Initiation*, (London, SPCK, 1965), p. 106.

82. J. D. C. Fisher, *Christian Initiation: Baptism in the Medieval West: A Study in the Disintegration of the Primitive Rite of Initiation*, (London, SPCK, 1965), p. 105.

83. J. D. C. Fisher, *Christian Initiation: Baptism in the Medieval West: A Study in the Disintegration of the Primitive Rite of Initiation*, (London, SPCK, 1965), p. 106.

84. J. D. C. Fisher, *Christian Initiation: Baptism in the Medieval West: A Study in the Disintegration of the Primitive Rite of Initiation*, (London, SPCK, 1965), p. 105.

85. T. E. Bridgett, *History of the Holy Eucharist in Great Britain, Vol. II*,. (London, C. Kegan Paul and Co., 1881), pp. 23-24.

86. J. D. C. Fisher, *Christian Initiation: Baptism in the Medieval West: A Study in the Disintegration of the Primitive Rite of Initiation*, (London, SPCK, 1965), p. 106.

87. W. H. Freestone, *The Sacrament Reserved, A Survey of the Practice of Reserving the Eucharist, with Special Reference to the Communion of the Sick, During the First Twelve Centuries*, (London, A. R. Mowbray and Milwaukee, (The Young Churchman Co., 1917), p. 179..

88. W. E. Scudamore, *Notitia Eucharistica*, (London, Rivingtons, 1872), p. 51.

89. J. D. C. Fisher, *Christian Initiation: Baptism in the Medieval West: A Study in the Disintegration of the Primitive Rite of Initiation*, (London, SPCK, 1965), p. 106.

Source Notes

90. Boniface Luykx, "Confirmation in Relation to the Eucharist," *Readings in Sacramental Theology*, edited by C. Stephen Sullivan (Englewood Cliffs, New Jersey, Prentice-Hall, 1964), p. 199.

91. J. Clement Bennington, *The Recipient of Confirmation, A Historical Synopsis and Commentary*, (Washington, D.C., The Catholic University of America Press, 1952), p. 20.

Children's Communion in a Divided Church

1. Paul F. Palmer, editor and commentator, *Sacraments and Worship, Liturgy and Doctrinal Development of Baptism, Confirmation, and the Eucharist, Vol. I*, p. 259.

2. Frank W. Klos, *Confirmation and First Communion*, (St. Louis, Augsburg Publishing House, Board of Publication of the Lutheran Church in America and Concordia Publishing House, 1968) p. 45. [See also William J. *McDonald*, editor-in-chief, *New Catholic Encyclopedia, Vol. 14*. (New York, McGraw Hill, 1967) p. 37.

3. Urban T. Holmes, *Young Children and the Eucharist*, (New York, The Seabury Press, 1973), p. 19.

4. Marian Bohen, *The Mystery of Confirmation, A Theology of the Sacrament*, (New York, Herder and Herder, 1963), p. 35.

5. Boniface Luykx, "Confirmation in Relation to the Eucharist," *Readings in Sacramental Theology*, edited by C. Stephen Sullivan (Englewood Cliffs, New Jersey, Prentice-Hall, 1964), p. 201.

6. Urban T. Holmes, III, *Young Children and the Eucharist*, (New York, The Seabury Press, 1973), p. 90-91 citing Francis Buckley, *Children and God: Communion, Confession, and Confirmation* (New York, Corpus Publications, 1970)..

7. Urban T. Holmes, III, *Confirmation, the Celebration of Maturity in Christ*, (New York, The Seabury Press, n.d.), pp. 28-29.

8. Urban T. Holmes, III, *Confirmation, the Celebration of Maturity in Christ*, (New York, The Seabury Press, n.d.), pp. 43-44.

9. Society for Promoting Christian Knowledge, *Confirmation or the Laying on of Hands, Vol. I*, (London, SPCK, 1926), pp. 62-66.

Source Notes

10. Society for Promoting Christian Knowledge, *Confirmation or the Laying on of Hands, Vol. I*, (London, SPCK, 1926), p. 98.

11. Robert M. Adamson, *The Christian Doctrine of the Lord's Supper*, (Edinburgh, T. T. Clark, 1905), p. 260.

12. Society for Promoting Christian Knowledge, *Confirmation or the Laying on of Hands, Vol. I*, (London, SPCK, 1926), p. 98.

13. Society for Promoting Christian Knowledge, *Confirmation or the Laying on of Hands, Vol. I*, (London, SPCK, 1926), p. 98.

14. W. E. Scudamore, *Notitia Eucharistica*, (London, Rivingtons, 1872), p. 77.

15. Robert M. Adamson, *The Christian Doctrine of the Lord's Supper*, (Edinburgh, T. T. Clark, 1905), pp. 260-261.

16. J. Mark M. Dalby, *Open Communion in the Church of England*, (London, Church Book Room Press, Ltd., 1959), p. 23.

17. W. E. Scudamore, *Notitia Eucharistica*, (London, Rivingtons, 1872), p.47.

18. John Johnson, *The Unbloody Sacrivice, and Altar Unveiled and Supported...*,(Oxford, John Henry Parker, 1847, first published in 1774), pp.523-524.

19. Jeremy Taylor, *The Worthy Communicant*, (London, William Pickering, 1853), pp. 153-154.

20. Jeremy Taylor, *The Worthy Communicant*, (London, William Pickering, 1853), p. 155.

21. Colin Alves, "Communion and Confirmation," *Confirmation Crisis*, (New York, The Seabury Press, 1968), pp. 56-57.

22. Colin Alves, "Communion and Confirmation," *Confirmation Crisis*, (New York, The Seabury Press, 1968), pp. 58.

23. J. D. C. Fisher, "History and Theology," *Confirmation Crisis*, (New York, The Seabury Press, 1968`) p. 43.

24. Urban T. Holmes, III, *Young Children and the Eucharist*, (New York, The Seabury Press, 1973), pp. 57-58.

Source Notes

25. John M. Hines, *By Water and the Holy Spirit, New Concepts of Baptism, Confirmation, and Communion*, (New York, The Seabury Press, 1973), p. 42.

26. Arthur C. Repp, *Confirmation in the Lutheran Church*, (St. Louis, Missouri, Concordia Publishing House, 1964), p. 18, citing *Formula of Mass and Communion for the Church of Wittenberg*, 1523.

27. Arthur C. Repp, *Confirmation in the Lutheran Church*, (St. Louis, Missouri, Concordia Publishing House, 1964), p. 18, citing *Formula of Mass and Communion for the Church of Wittenberg*, 1523.

28. Frank W. Klos, *Confirmation and First Communion*, (St. Louis, Augsburg Publishing House, Board of Publication of the Lutheran Church in America and Concordia Publishing House, 1968), p. 188-190.

29. Commission on Education of the Lutheran World Federation, translated by Walter G. Tillmanns, *Confirmation: A StudyDocument*, (Minneapolis, Augsburg Publishing House, 1963), pp. 34-35.

30. Frank W. Klos, *Confirmation and First Communion*, (St. Louis, Augsburg Publishing House, Board of Publication of the Lutheran Church in America and Concordia Publishing House, 1968), p. 105.

31. Arthur C. Repp, *Confirmation in the Lutheran Church*, (St. Louis, Missouri, Concordia Publishing House, 1964), p. 56.

32. Arthur C. Repp, *Confirmation in the Lutheran Church*, (St. Louis, Missouri, Concordia Publishing House, 1964), p. 125.

33. Arthur C. Repp, *Confirmation in the Lutheran Church*, (St. Louis, Missouri, Concordia Publishing House, 1964), p. 126.

34. Arthur C. Repp, *Confirmation in the Lutheran Church*, (St. Louis, Missouri, Concordia Publishing House, 1964), pp. 144-145.

35. Frank W. Klos, *Confirmation and First Communion*, (St. Louis, Augsburg Publishing House, Board of Publication of the Lutheran Church in America and Concordia Publishing House, 1968), p. 199.

Source Notes

36. Arthur C. Repp, *Confirmation in the Lutheran Church*, (St. Louis, Missouri, Concordia Publishing House, 1964), p. 49.

37. Robert M. Adamson, *The Christian Doctrine of the Lord's Supper*, (Edinburgh, T. T. Clark, 1905), p. 261.

38. George B. Burnet, *The Holy Communion in the Reformed Church of Scotland, 1560-1960*, (Edinburgh and London, Oliver and Boyd, 1960), p. 46.

39. George B. Burnet, *The Holy Communion in the Reformed Church of Scotland, 1560-1960*, (Edinburgh and London, Oliver and Boyd, 1960), p. 46.

40. George B. Burnet, *The Holy Communion in the Reformed Church of Scotland, 1560-1960*, (Edinburgh and London, Oliver and Boyd, 1960), p. 56.

41. George B. Burnet, *The Holy Communion in the Reformed Church of Scotland, 1560-1960*, (Edinburgh and London, Oliver and Boyd, 1960), p. 283.

42. George B. Burnet, *The Holy Communion in the Reformed Church of Scotland, 1560-1960*, (Edinburgh and London, Oliver and Boyd, 1960), p. 283.

43. George B. Burnet, *The Holy Communion in the Reformed Church of Scotland, 1560-1960*, (Edinburgh and London, Oliver and Boyd, 1960), p. 168.

44. Hartzler, *The Educational Function of Developmental Rites, (New Haven, Conn., unpublished PhD dissertation at Yale University,1959), p. 260, citing* Emil Handiger and E. Tenfel, "Confirmation," *The Mennonite Encyclopedia, Vol. I*, p. 686.

45. *Westminster Confession of Faith*, cited by MacNaughton, ed., *Power to Permit, Children at the Lord's Supper*, (Board of Christian Education, United Presbyterian Church in the United States of America, undated publication), p. 5.

46. *Westminster Confession of Faith*, cited by MacNaughton, ed., *Power to Permit, Children at the Lord's Supper*, (Board of Christian Education, United Presbyterian Church in the United States of America, undated publication), p. 1.